An introduction to

POLYMER PAINTING

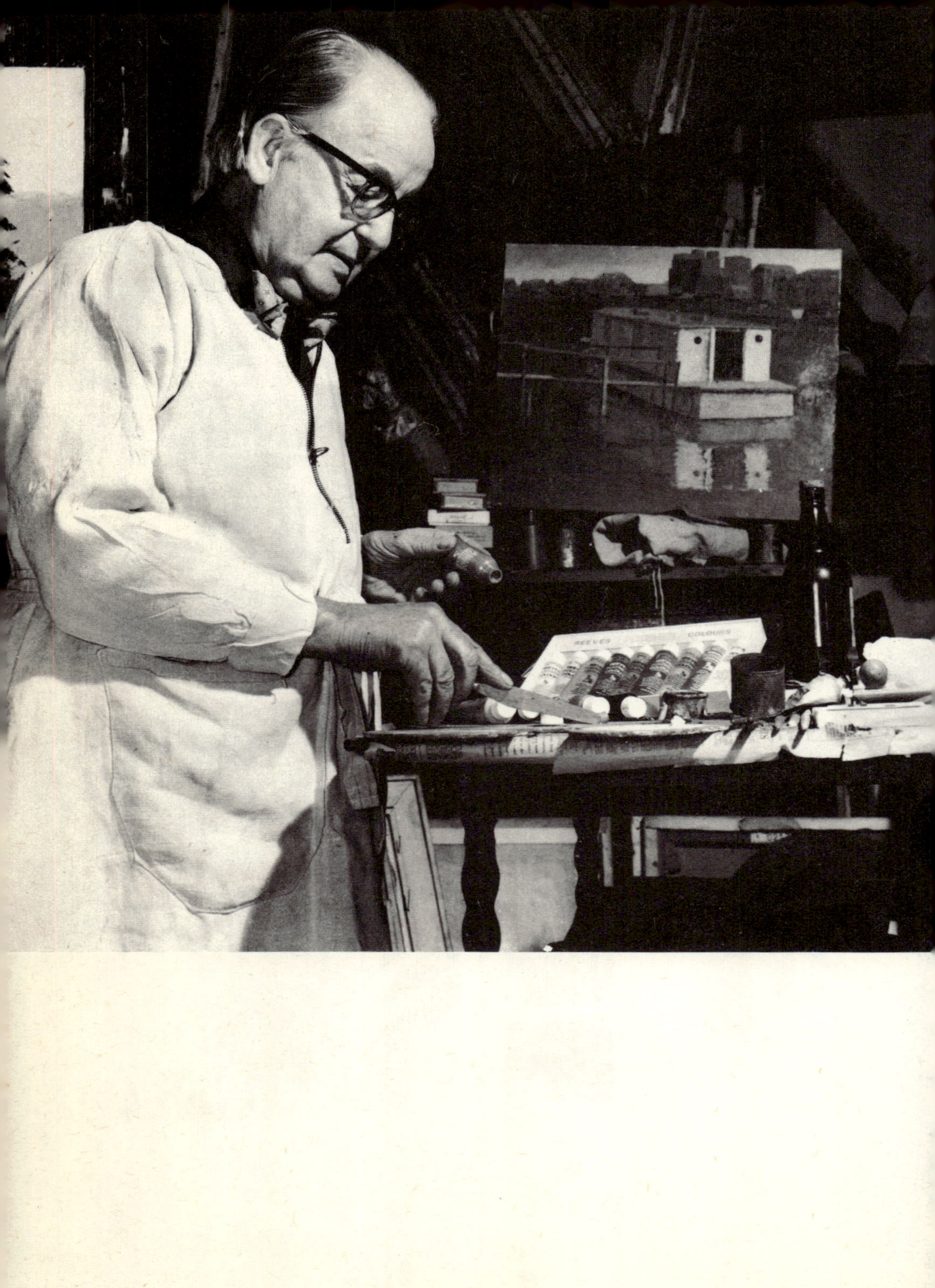
REEVES
COLOURS

An introduction to

POLYMER PAINTING

by

HAROLD WORKMAN

R.B.A., R.O.I., R.C.A., R.S.M.A.

LONDON

BLANDFORD PRESS

167 High Holborn, London, WC1

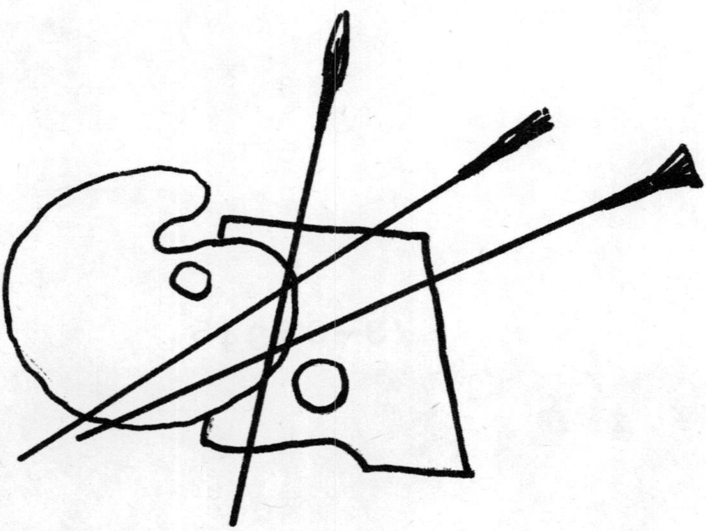

Printed in Great Britain by
Jarrold and Sons Ltd, Norwich

CONTENTS

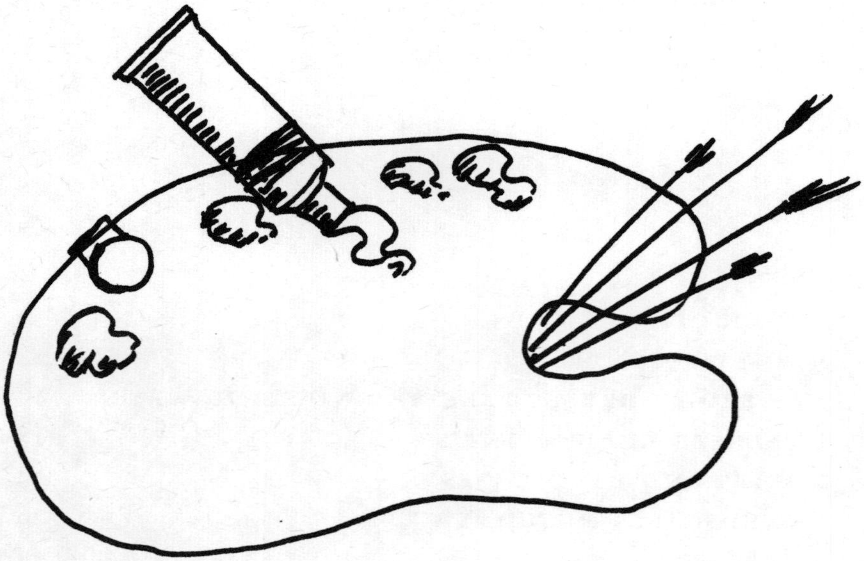

INTRODUCTION

Sometimes we are only concerned with the objective approach to our favourite subject and seldom does the student depart from the convention of painting an accurate picture of the scene before him. For a time satisfaction is assured. But sooner or later inward stirrings or restlessness create an urge to journey forth to new regions of expression. This has applied to almost every artist; he feels a great desire for something more to say without submerging his own personal expression and becoming eccentric. This would be only a form of unpleasant exhibitionism destroying any inherent talent previously shown.

The answer then is a more progressive journey towards perfection without destroying the personality. Possibly development can be achieved by a different approach to a composition – by changing the perspective, by changing the mood of the prevailing light or by the introduction of an exciting new medium. To continue with the same medium whether it is oil, watercolour or gouache without trying a new medium is like a bird struggling to fly with only one wing. One will continue travelling round in circles without knowing what lies ahead. Admittedly a journey in unexplored territory presents lots of surprises – some may have sad moments, but others may be very exciting.

This is the road to development, instead of always lavishly reproducing the same sort of subject.

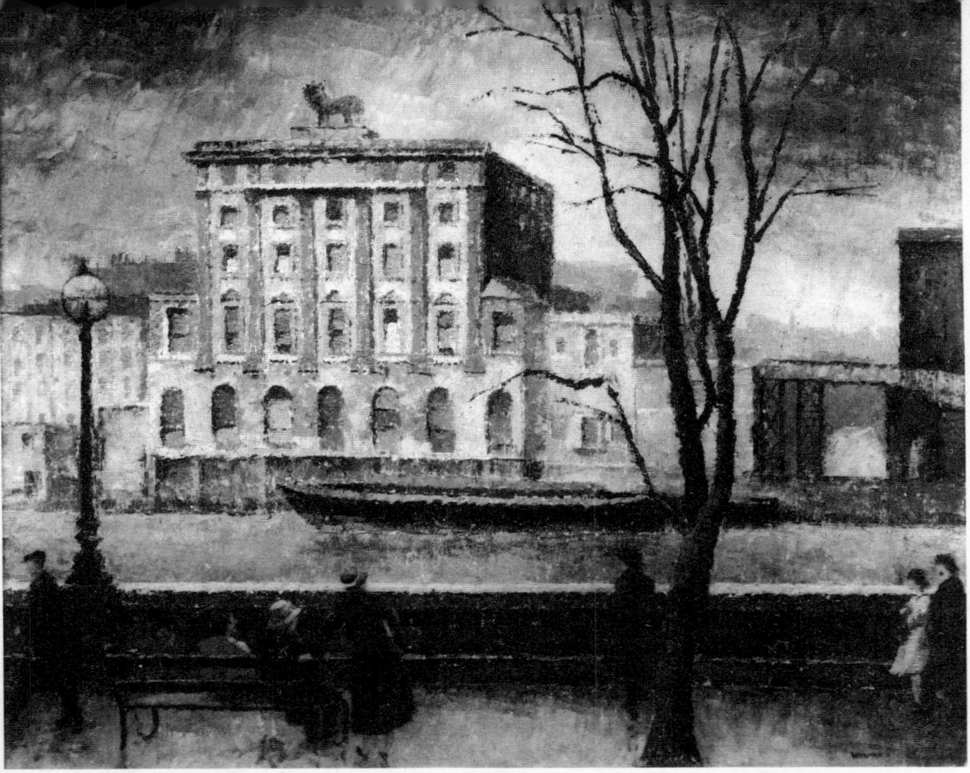

'The Old Red Lion Brewery'—Formerly on the South Bank but now destroyed to give space for the Festival Hall

With the adventure of using a new medium the pictures of the artist will still reveal his own personal touch. His fuller understanding of the new Polymer will assist him to adapt his working-out of the subject and preserve the individual appreciation of the pictorial subject. In endeavouring to master a directive in the use of the new medium there is no need to interfere with the artist's facility, style or vision which will not be clouded in any way by the new technical change but rather assisted in its new development. It merely enlarges the artist's horizon.

Painting is not only an expression of the senses but is also associated with the required skill in learning how to use the new paints rather than an instant dismissal of their possibilities, for they will assist the artist to create the pictures that he desires to illustrate. The required skill, however, should not be allowed to impede the aesthetic selectivity of the artist because the new medium demands a modern or unorthodox approach.

1 A cloud study using Phthalo blue, Phthalo green, Burnt umber, Cadmium red, and Titanium white

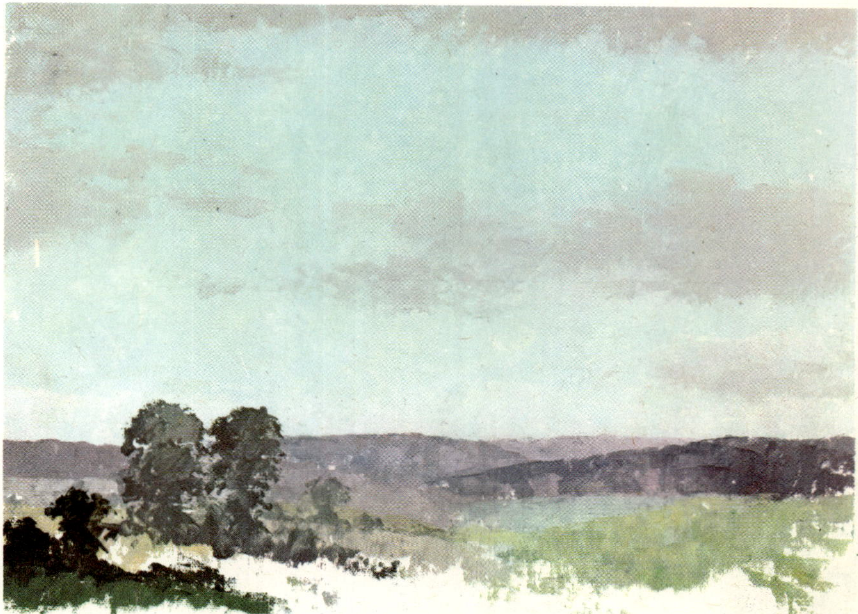

2 A sky and cloud study in afternoon light about an hour before sunset. The colour relationship between the clouds and the distant hills is recognisable

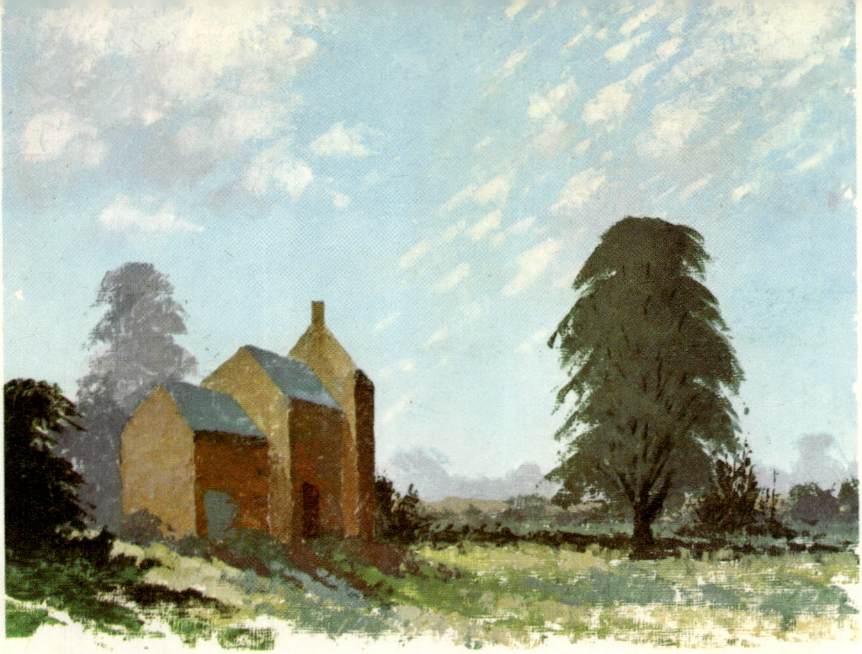

3 An East Anglian farmstead, using grained oil sketching paper. Applied with a palette knife

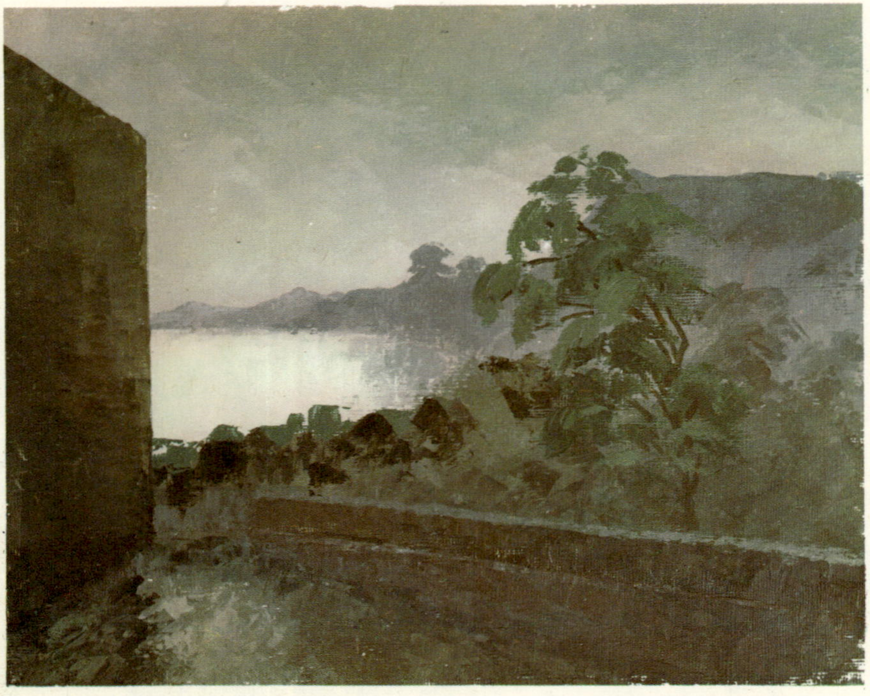

4 A wet day painted in Bangor, N. Wales. Using a limited palette, Phthalo blue, Green, and Burnt umber. Derivations from these colours will produce the greys seen on a wet day

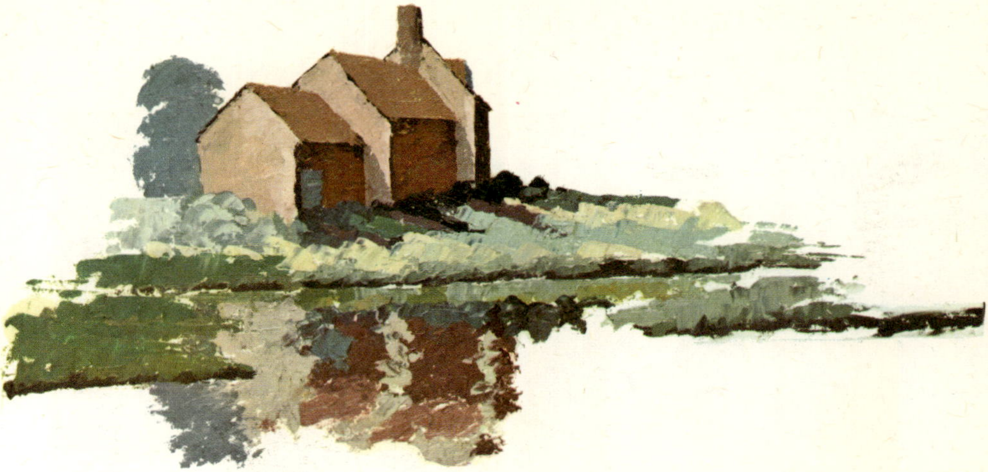

5 TOP: *Reflections in a farm pond of a cluster of buildings in sunlight. The colours used were Alizarin crimson, Yellow ochre, Phthalo green, Burnt umber, and White*

6 LEFT: *Tree study using Phthalo blue, Burnt umber, Yellow ochre and White, using varied knife-strokes*

7 BELOW: *Sketch of a bush using Phthalo blue, Phthalo green, Yellow ochre, and White, using varied knife-strokes*

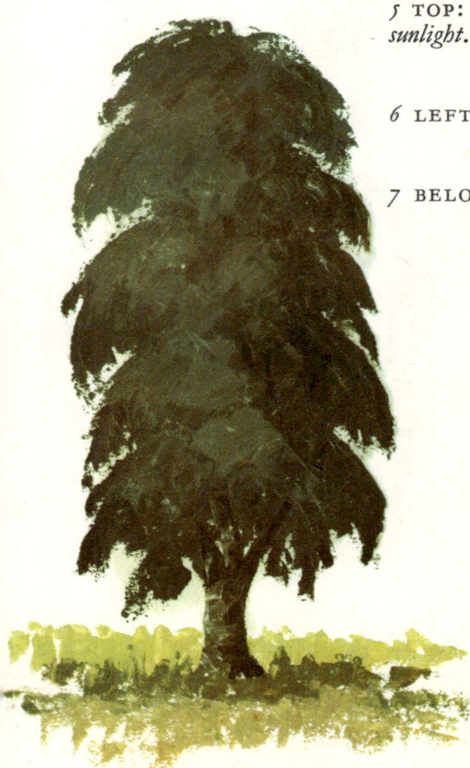

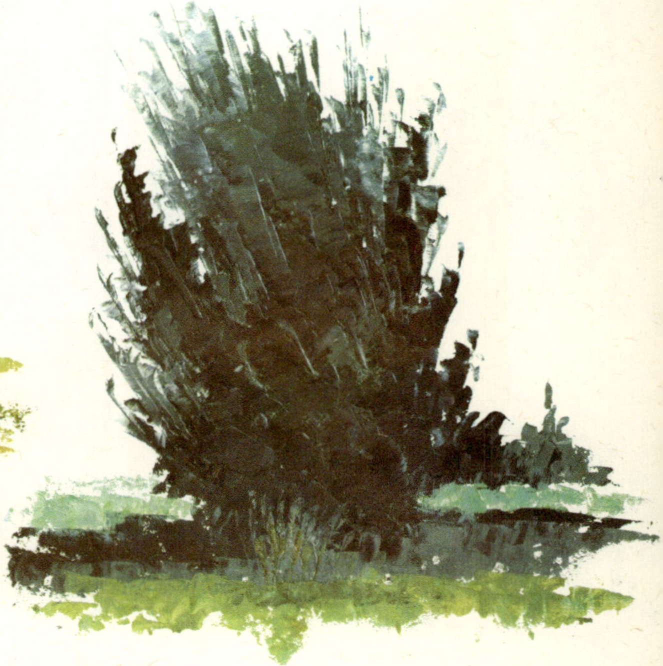

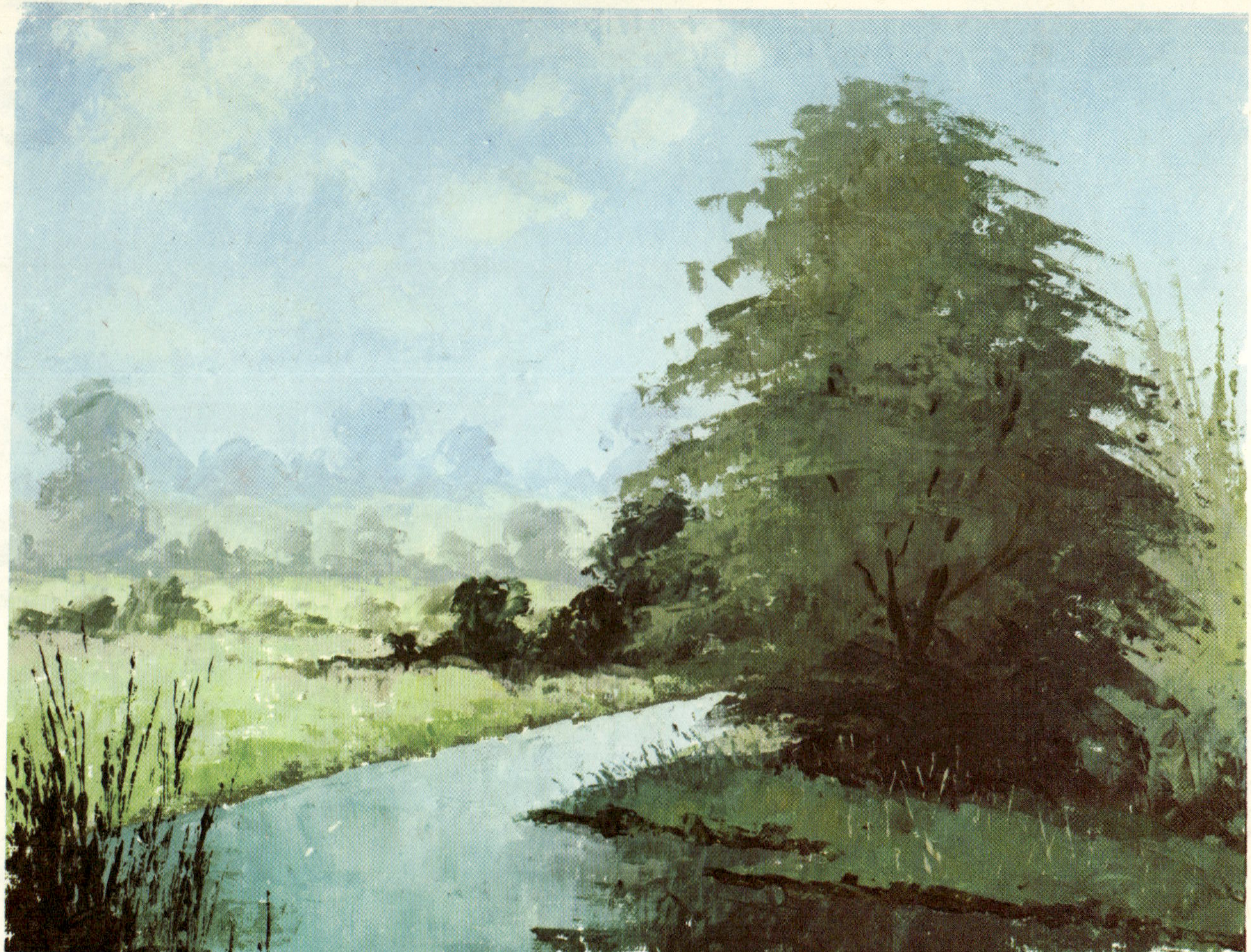

8 A river sketch near Norwich where the colours were made from Phthalo blue, Phthalo green, Yellow ochre, Burnt umber, and Titanium white. The long dark rushes assist the balance of tone. Using a palette knife in various types of stroke

The past or present generations are often closely associated with what is only possible by what has already been achieved in any accepted medium. This springs from the slowness of the average mind to adapt itself to another medium and sometimes a new angle of vision. The paintings which are still accepted as objective or realistic art when executed in previously understood methods create a restlessness in the more sophisticated individual and leave a feeling of lifelessness in this exciting new world.

There is no danger in any well-tried technical application but to some the regimentation could be easily lamented especially when the watercolour washes go wrong and become unmanageable, or the oils take so long to dry making it more difficult to apply more pigment and to carry the wet canvas home after painting out of doors.

No wonder there are so many artists who are satisfied to follow the well-trodden path rather than try a new method which will break away from the conventional, or enlarge it, introducing new visions and increasing the facility of the artist and so preventing any sterility in his work.

Without this new approach, however satisfactory the old method may have been, the work could degenerate and become a mechanical formula where all vital force is lost. Is it not far better to be courageous and tackle the new medium and make the work more of an adventure?

Composition in Norfolk. The horizontal hedges help the illusion of the flat fields of the landscape

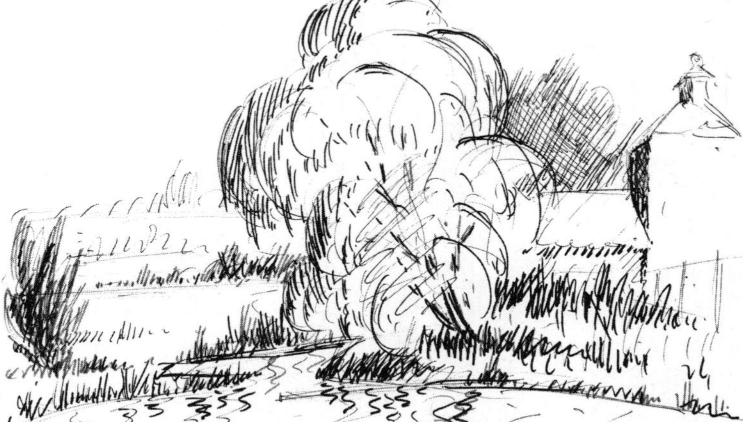

1 WHAT POLYMER IS

Nothing is stationary, everything is moving, developing and providing new materials to meet the requirements of this new age – new pigments to add to the already long list of artist's requirements, all very important to the growing need of the painter.

Among several recent new mediums the introduction of Polymer is of particular interest to the painter of today. So let us examine what this new pigment is.

Firstly, it has a range of colours similar to those found in most usual oils or watercolours because the same permanent pigments are used in the manufacture.

Secondly, instead of the colours being ground in oil as in the case of oil colours, these are ground in an Acrylic resin similar to that used in the manufacture of commercial materials including various types of Polythene and Perspex, etc.

Thirdly, the resulting pigment is fully permanent and intermixable. It is unchanging in drying. In the case of some opaque colours it is usually paler when dry. It is also firm and will not lift or move when a fresh layer of colour is used. It will not crack or change in colour value in the process of ageing.

During mixing and application only water is needed to dilute it or to keep it manageable during the period of using it.

Although Polymer is mixed with water it should not be associated with watercolour pigment, neither should it be considered with oil colour. All three are different and have their own uses and none of them will replace the others. Each fulfils its own part and is important for different reasons. Each forms part of an artist's equipment giving the widest possible range to his endeavours.

The pigment may be applied thinly with a brush, using only water to dilute it, when it will be found to be slower in drying. It may also be used to cover thinly a canvas or board to prepare a coloured ground for painting in the ordinary way with oil colours. This need only be done about twenty minutes before beginning the painting.

Palette knife painting – when only a small amount of water is added to the pigment – is particularly successful with Polymer especially as the knife is so easily cleaned on a rag during painting.

For outdoor sketching the fast-drying nature of the pigment will be found to be an advantage when an artist wishes to add more detail to his sketch as this is easily carried out when the under painting is partially dry and there is no fear of mixing with the previous colour. The quicker drying painting is easier to transport than one which would remain wet for a couple of days.

Unlike oil pigments, these colours have more flexibility and do not change in their character with the passing of time; whereas in the case of oil colours – because of the oils used in mixing – they are more likely to change with age. It is also understood that certain oil colours may be somewhat fugitive whereas the Polymer colours are all permanent.

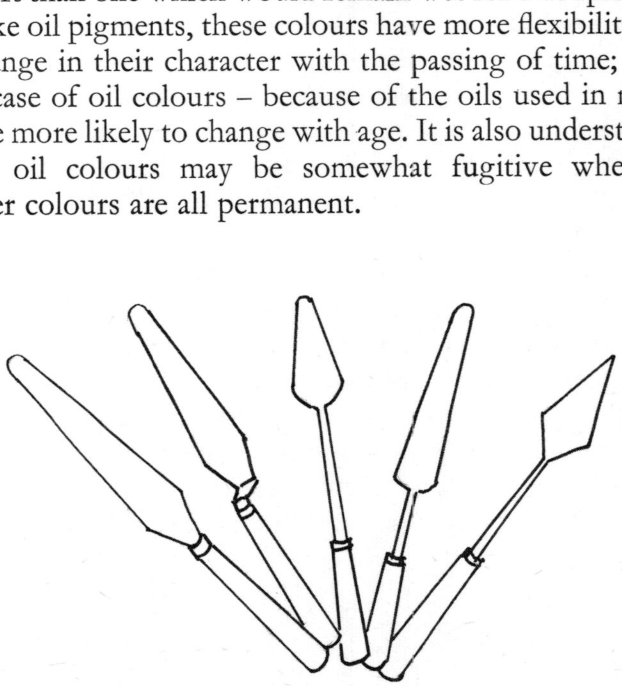

2 *METHODS: BRUSH, PALETTE KNIFE AND WASH*

Artists have always worked many different ways and mixed many mediums with their different pigments. These substances used for mixing pigments have been known as binders and according to the different liquids the finished pigment would be used for different purposes. In watercolour the binder would be a type of glue or glycerine. For tempera painting egg-yolk would be used to mix the different pigments, and in the case of oils various oils would be used according to the tone value of the pigment or colour to be used for grinding. In fresco painting only lime water is used to hold the dry colour together whilst it is painted on to a wet plaster surface, thus the colour, though limited in its colour range – owing to the use of lime – becomes part of the surface of the wall and has proved to be permanent in the countries where it has been used.

Artists have always sought new methods when a different proposition presents itself. The various supports that the artist used for his painting required the utmost care in the preparation used, as unfortunate results occurred if the surface was incorrect. A common fault with an incorrect or too brittle priming would result in cracking, therefore care in priming is important in most types of painting. In the case of the new Polymer paints the danger of incorrect grounds causing cracking and fading is now eliminated. By merely using a thin application of the colour or white, as the case may be, and mixing with water a satisfactory surface is found. Supports such as hardboard, Essex board, paper or cloth will respond to this treatment, and because of the nature of the resin used in the manufacture of this Polymer emulsion it will not crack and it also remains permanent. Therefore these emulsion-based colours have numerous advantages for the painter, especially as only water is required for dilution. They should not be mixed with oil colours, turps or oil, and it is not advisable to mix with another type of emulsion paint as a different resin has probably been used. This would cause the colour to thicken and reduce its flowing power. The flow property of the medium is very important and allows the artist to use either a knife or different types of brushes with complete freedom. Unlike oil pigment, emulsion paints will retain sufficient flexibility to prevent cracking even when rolled up, and in years to come will remain permanent and retain their richness of colour. Exhaustive tests give complete confidence in their permanence and Polymer resins will withstand the long period of time.

When using brushes, they should be constantly rinsed in water to prevent the pigment hardening in the bristles. They should not be left standing in water but always laid flat when not in use.

Palette knife painting is probably easiest to handle as this needs only wiping on a rag when changing the colour or when the knife becomes coated.

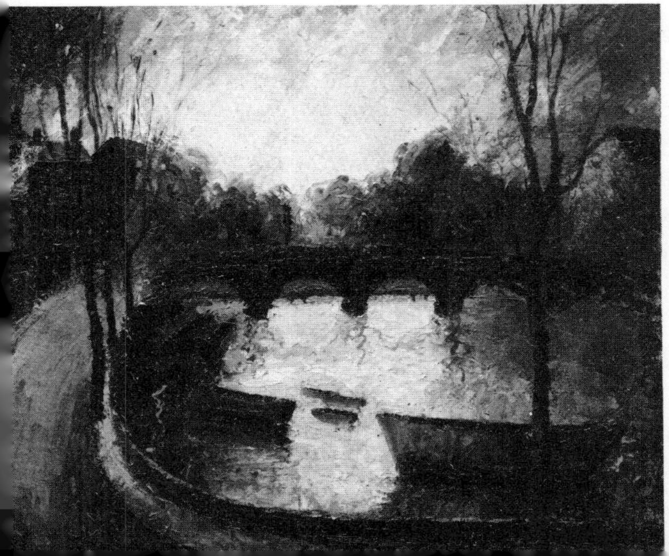

'Departing Night, Chelsea'— In the collection of Mrs. L. Leuchars, Durban

3 | *PALETTE KNIFE PAINTING*

Having briefly described the different manufacture of the various media compared with the Polymer pigment, we shall describe the use of the palette knife in applying this new pigment; but in endeavouring to instruct and illustrate the merits of Polymer paint with palette knife painting it is not intended to defend it as the only method of expression but one that should be added to the general study of painting. As in other forms of Art, emulsion painting can be used to enjoy the expression of either an objective, figurative or modern approach whilst keeping it free from such things as intellectual prejudices which immediately create barriers, thus preventing a clearer appreciation of its object.

It is important that the artist's enthusiasm to paint a subject should begin as an emotional approach towards a composition and urged by the desire for expression in a medium which will re-enforce his conviction towards success in the chosen pigment.

Some students are constantly experimenting with various types of pigments and supports, yet others are quite satisfied with the use of one sort of pigment, thus turning their development into some sort of cul-de-sac. It is, however, for those who seek a fuller understanding of the possibilities of the Polymer colours that this book is intended, to help along their journey.

As this new paint dries more quickly than oil colour, over-painting may be done in about half an hour without disturbing the previous surface. Also by the addition of water the drying can be held back whilst the painting of 'wet into wet' is carried out. This particularly applies to the painting of skies and clouds.

We must appreciate that the speed of drying of this pigment can be an advantage when one wants to take a sketch home after outdoor painting. This, then, is the end of all the artist's troubles in returning home with a wet canvas besides waiting several days for the paint to dry. We also find that our oil painting looks uneven when it has dried because of the 'sinking' of certain paints. What is known as 'oiling out' is therefore required to restore the dark tones to their full value and before any further over-painting can be carried out.

In the case of Polymer all the colours dry quite evenly and any further paint applied to the dry surface does not show nor does it appear to present a crumby appearance.

Incidentally one does not require any turpentine, oil or varnish. Water only is needed for thinning, but because of the fugitive nature of the pigment and its hardening always remember to replace the caps on the tubes after use.

Many materials with suitable surfaces can be used for this kind of painting and some, such as oil sketching paper, are quite cheap. If, however, you prefer to make your own, this can be done by buying a roll of canvas-grained lining paper and preparing this with a mixture of a tablespoonful of powdered gelatine and the same quantity of plaster of Paris mixed with a half pint of boiling water. Essex board is also suitable but in this case the priming should be applied on both sides and the edges, as this will prevent it from bending. Next is any type of hardboard, but because there is no tendency to twist it is not necessary to prepare both sides. Most people prefer to paint on the smooth side and adjust the mixture of the preparation – by increasing the amount of plaster – to suit their particular type of work. The rough side of the board is usually found to be too rough and, besides taking more pigment, it also dictates the result to the painter, while the smooth side allows the artist to make his own adjustments regarding the desired texture.

Hardboard may also be used for covering with such fabrics as butter muslin which can be stuck down with a mixture of ordinary glue size. When dry it should be prepared with the above preparation.

For those who prefer the feel of the more expensive product there is a canvas stretcher or a canvas-covered board.

The illustrations were carried out on the latter type board and mainly a palette knife was used.

Contrary to what some people believe, knife painting need not require more pigment than is normally used with brushes. Apart from those who usually paint with a very thick impasto, there is no need to load the canvas heavily with paint making it look like a relief map. If thicker technique is required this would be reserved for objects in the foreground which would then help the recession of the subject and impart a feeling of space.

Having decided to use, say, two knives, whether they be pear-shaped, the cranked handle type or a straight palette knife, any of these should be enough to express all the pattern and movement one would require.

For the palette, porcelain, glass or Perspex are found to be most suitable as all are non-absorbent, unlike wood, which is more difficult to clean.

In this book it is hoped to give some practical advice to the students who require professional guidance on palette knife painting. It will be generally agreed that to the uninitiated this form of expression does constitute one of the most difficult forms of painting. Even the very thought of putting paint on canvas with anything except lots of brushes immediately strikes the student with terror. Yet it is hoped to show that one can quickly learn how to achieve the most exciting compositions and textures in various forms of expression with a couple of knives instead of a dozen or more brushes.

Clean tools always help to produce the best work. Therefore always wipe your knives after use as any painting knife which is covered with dried paint will not work so well as a clean metal surface. Quite often a student has produced a palette knife covered with hard dried-up paint – which destroys the flexibility

– and still expected to compose a painting with such a rough surface. When the flexibility is reduced it limits the manœuvrability which is so important in work of this kind. In fact they may as well try to paint with a hard kitchen knife! I remember one student arriving in my studio with such a knife and being surprised that it proved difficult to paint a picture. Admittedly she was painting with a knife. But oh, what a result: even the palette was too small, which added to the difficulties with such an insensitive knife.

To achieve success the student should have some knowledge of draughtsmanship, perspective and composition and an understanding of the atmosphere of the particular subject whether it is architectural, landscape, marine or still-life that is being painted. There is a sort of 'personality' with most subjects which contributes towards the impact that the work achieves. These great heights of achievement, the object of our ultimate ambition, will lead us through indefinable paths, each according to his own personality, reaching out unhindered, and enjoying the full advantages of pigment and palette knife – expressing in full the composition and rhythmic assembly of form.

Should an elementary knowledge of drawing and perspective be completely absent, it is advisable for the student first to gain some proficiency in general drawing before beginning to paint. Although an artist will deliberately lose a line in the process of painting with the palette knife, the original basis of construction can always be restored when required. This is described as losing and finding the line and keeping the design fluid which is often helpful in the ultimate rhythm of the subject.

One cannot stress too strongly the need for this basic knowledge of draughtsmanship as it must be a heart-breaking experience for a student to waste his work because he does not know that the drawing is wrong; all the painting in the world will not turn a bad drawing into a good subject.

4 SKIES AND LANDSCAPES

It is advisable at first not to try to emulate the compositions of a great master, but instead to begin in a simple way which will provide the best basis for progressive development.

First we shall use only a few colours for our study of skies, clouds and landscapes. These will be Phthalo blue, Phthalo green, Cadmium red, Burnt umber, Yellow ochre and Titanium white. This list of colours will be enough for the beginner for a subject of this kind.

Place a few drops of water on each place where the spots of colour are to be placed. Use the back edge of the palette for squeezing out a small amount of colour, about the same quantity as you would use along the length of a toothbrush – you can always increase this when required – and next drop a few spots of water on each pigment, this will help to keep the Polymer moist during use. Next try out your knives with the paint using the middle of the palette for mixing and place a few drops of water on the part where the paint will be mixed. An old tumbler is best to hold the water and it will be found that when the knife is dipped into the water it will pick up enough to shake on to the palette. First pick up a little thin paint with the edge of the knife and lightly touch the canvas with the edge. This will show you how to make thin lines which can be varied according to the amount of paint you pick up. This is used for expressing such things as fences, ropes, masts of boats or branches of trees.

The flat surfaces can be applied by using about half the length of the knife and spreading the paint on the surface like putting butter on bread, but remember to spread the paint and not to leave it in patches when skies are being painted as these knife strokes should overlap to produce a flat surface before the clouds are introduced.

Plate 1

Skies should always be painted first, beginning at the top of the canvas with a mixture of Phthalo blue and white to the desired shade and covering about two inches in depth. The colour is now made a shade lighter with white and a small fragment of green added to continue the next two inches. After this the same change is made until the horizon is reached, which should now be much paler and produce a sense of recession as is found in most sky studies. The clouds are next introduced and, painting the shade side first, which is a mixture of white plus a little blue and red, the flat of the knife is still used to produce a broad and loose effect. After this the light part is added which is made from a mixture of white with a small touch of burnt umber. The distant trees or the far-away hills will often be derived from the colour of the shade side of the clouds.

In the study of clouds one sees a play of light and colour which is readily identifiable with the angle of incidence or the play of light. Observe the shade side of the cloud in relation to that part which is influenced by the prevailing light. Note also the comparative tone value of the distant details which are all interrelated with what is above.

By constant observation one will certainly accumulate a knowledge and understanding of colour and tone which will prove invaluable and readily applicable in direct painting for objective compositions.

The development of one's observation is of the utmost importance. This cannot be over-emphasised. The eye of the artist must be ever open, whether he is a landscape painter,

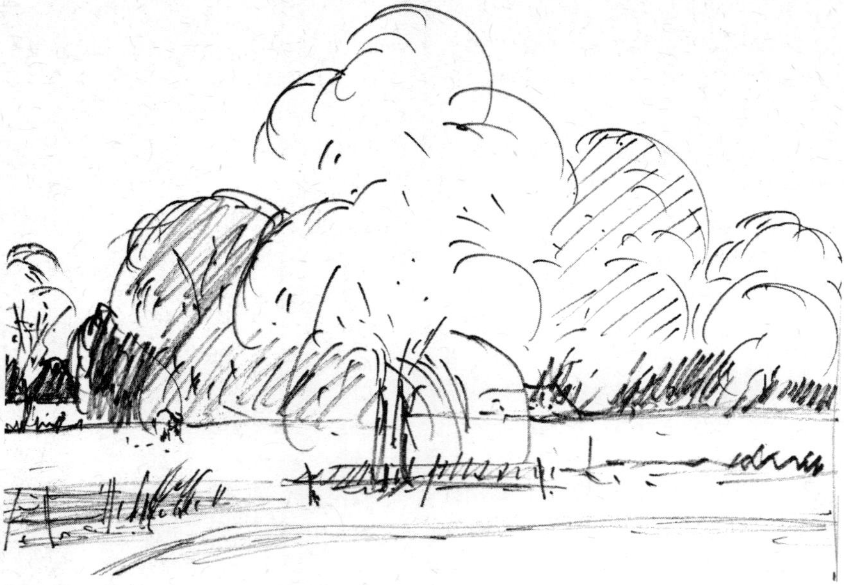

'Trees near Norwich'—Rhythmic shapes in foliage. Note the introduction of the dark shapes in the distance which enables the lighter greens to be appreciated

flower painter or still-life painter, the same rule applies. In the process of the student's development he should be conscious of the tone of the subject, where the lights and darks are introduced, and the effect produced by them: the next stage is to see the composition in terms of colour and thus he is preparing himself for an expression in a direct approach. This means the ability to paint one passage in its correct colour value and every other part will follow in the same direct way, owing its value to the colour already stated. Thus there is an absence of fumbling or trial-and-error because the mind has first been swept clean of any uncertainties by the first study of the subject, after which one is more prepared for a positive and direct approach.

Plate 2

The partially finished landscape in a late afternoon light was treated with more warmth in the colours. The sky colour was mixed with more green added and in the simple evening clouds a little more red was introduced into the colour and the distant hills were treated with an equally warm colour which associated itself with the warm cloud colour.

Plate 3

The cloud pattern shows a different arrangement of shapes suitable for the farm buildings subject. A wider range of colour was employed especially with the slate roofs and the brick structure of the farm, whilst a much more extensive range of greens was included in the country landscape. The dark greens used in the bushes and trees were made from Phthalo blue and Burnt umber with white for the medium tones, and for the darkest values in the foreground the blue and Burnt umber without white was used. The greens in the fields were made from white, Phthalo green and Yellow ochre and within this range all the different shades of green were obtained.

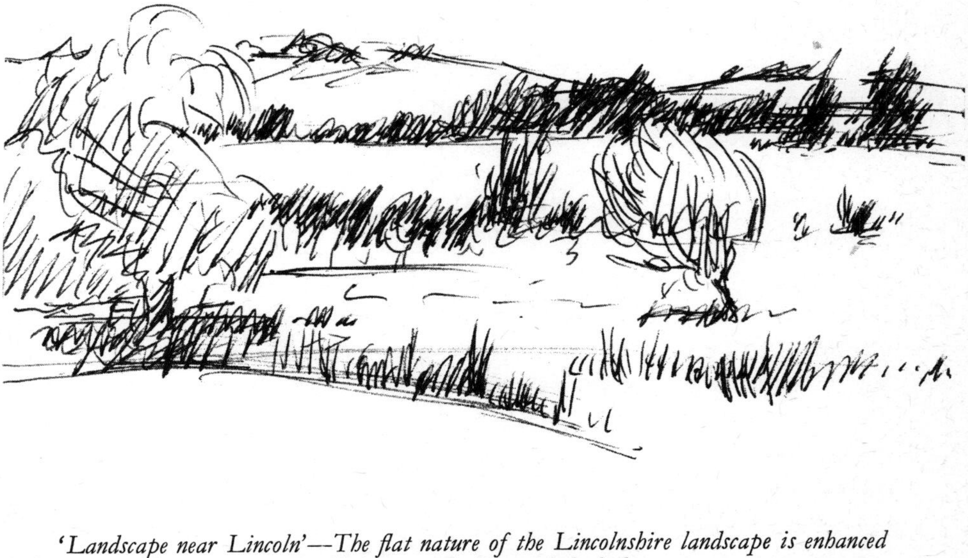

'Landscape near Lincoln'—The flat nature of the Lincolnshire landscape is enhanced by the horizontal shapes of the hedges

5 LANDSCAPES IN SUMMER

The fragmentary details shown in Plates 5, 6 and 7 will be found helpful when you begin to paint a complete landscape. For instance the technique for putting on the paint for painting trees of different shapes is shown; naturally there is a limit to the number of shapes to be shown but these should be sufficient to begin with. One type of tree shows the bunches of foliage falling downwards, therefore the knife-strokes should follow in the same way, putting in the darker tones first and adding the lighter tones afterwards, always noting how the bunches of the growth catch the light in order to illustrate the roundness of the tree. At the same time one must observe the outside edges of the tree against the sky; particularly the shapes of the spaces behind the foliage so that it does not appear solid and shapeless.

Another type of bush or tree is clearly demonstrated in Plate 7 where the knife-edge strokes are again expressive, showing the growth and volume of the wayside bush frequently found in the countryside. Care should be taken to notice the upward direction of the growth of the tree as opposed to the downward and round strokes shown in Plate 6. The training of one's observation in this respect is as important as the development of the facility with the use of the knife.

The details to be shown in Plate 5 show the method of expressing certain patterns and shapes to be found in the foreground of many country scenes. As these passages are shown in this particular way it should be easier to appreciate the method of application in this subject. The tree and buildings shown against the sky are illustrated reflected in the pond in the foreground where the colour of the reflections is adjusted to the local colour of the water, and the slight movement of the water. Provided there is not a wind present to disturb the surface of the water – in which case the colour will be more derivative from the sky colour – the water will show the reflections in reverse of what is shown above and which will be influenced by the colour of the water. The colour value of waterways differs considerably and therefore the reflections are accordingly influenced by the colour change. Extremely clear water will show reflections to almost the same value as the objects above, while dirty water, whether it is brownish or dark green will be influenced by absorbing the colour of the water and thus reducing the intensity of the pure colours to be seen reflected. A safe rule to follow in this respect is to note that the reflection of light colours is slightly darker and the dark are seen to be slightly lighter. In other words they become more muted together as they would appear if viewed through coloured glasses which would represent the value of the water; therefore if one imagined a view through various lenses each would produce a different effect as would be seen when the reflections were absorbed by the various types of water.

If water should be introduced diminishing into the perspective, as in the case of a river, it will be found that the distant part of the water is lighter as it would be derivative from the horizon colour of the sky: while the near part of the water would be darker and influenced by the sky immediately above except where objects near by are reflected.

The calligraphy of the knife is best introduced, using perpendicular strokes and not horizontal ones. This method helps to introduce any movement to be seen in water.

The river subject shown in Plate 8 illustrates the effect of light on the receding water, and the change of values in the colours of the trees in the landscape shows how the intensity of the greens changes as each area disappears as it is absorbed into the atmosphere on the distant horizon.

A simple landscape as illustrated in Plate 9 is another indication where the play of light will produce different effects on a subject. Sometimes when the sun is passing behind a cloud some parts of the subject are thrown in shadow, providing a more dramatic effect, as is the case with the colour of the distant hills in this composition. Nevertheless, although the tone of these hills is dark they are just a darker version of the same colour which was used in the shade side of the clouds.

The dramatic content of the subject is further amplified by the rich dark contrast of the trees against the summer sky.

While we are dealing with general instructions in this method of painting it does not follow that everyone will paint the same. Indeed it is not so. That is the last thing we want. There is no intention to destroy or interfere with the personality in each artist's work, but rather to assist his own development towards his own personal success. Just as all people are different in their various ways it will necessarily follow that everyone's work will ultimately show something of the artist's personality, plus any reaction they receive from the subject, unless they are satisfied always to remain eclectic, with no personal vision of their own.

Psychologically and theoretically it should be possible to identify the type of work executed by any artist provided that it is original. The timid or weak person can be seen just as clearly as a more adventurous and vigorous type. The choice of colours and the texture of his work give as fair an indication of the hesitancy or originality of the artist's approach as does the consistency of his work.

This is probably more easily identified in palette knife work than in painting with brushes; therefore the verve and joy that is felt with this work will greatly assist in the liberation of the artist's personality and thus reach out to added expression.

Whether the subject be landscape, still-life or flowers, all must have certain things in common. They should have good colour – this may be low-toned harmony or high-keyed contrast – good composition and attractive technique, joyous and exciting, apart

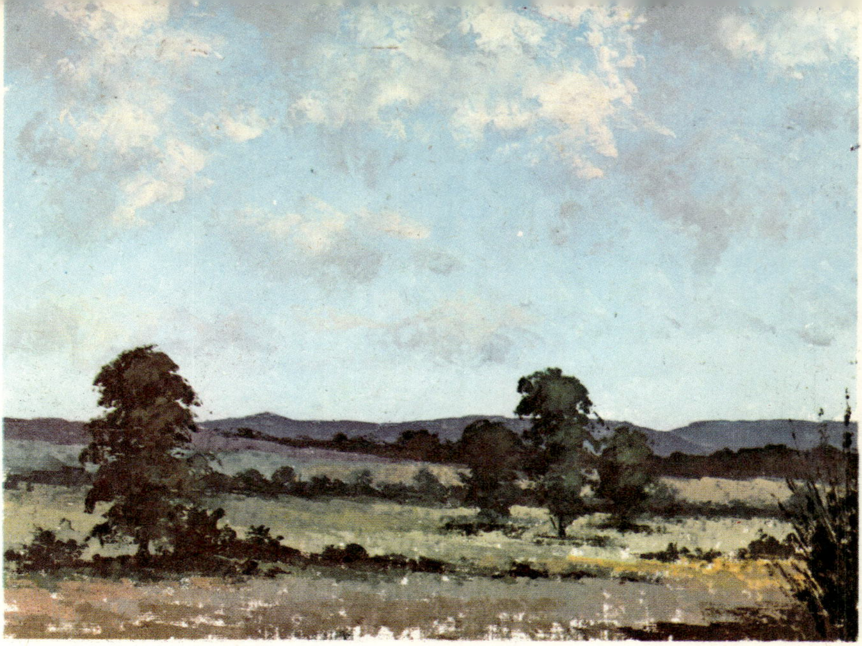

9 This sketch of a Surrey landscape was done in the afternoon sunlight where the angle of the sun allowed the distant landscape to appear rich and dark against the sky, thus increasing the strength of light in the sky

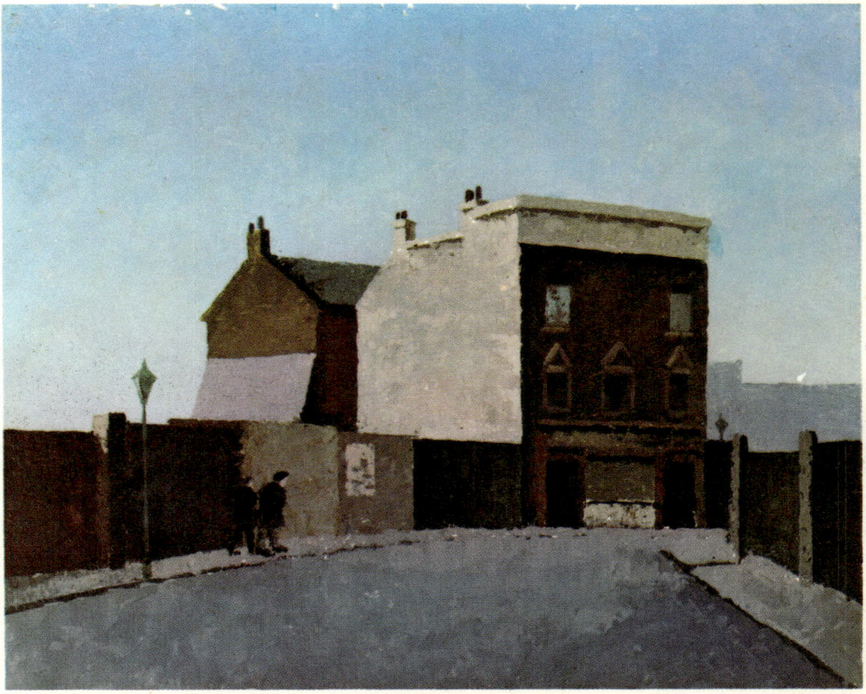

10 The Prospect of Whitby, Wapping. This historic hostelry, famous in Stepney, where seamen have gathered for hundreds of years, is now embodied in an arrangement of classical shapes and colour worthy of its background

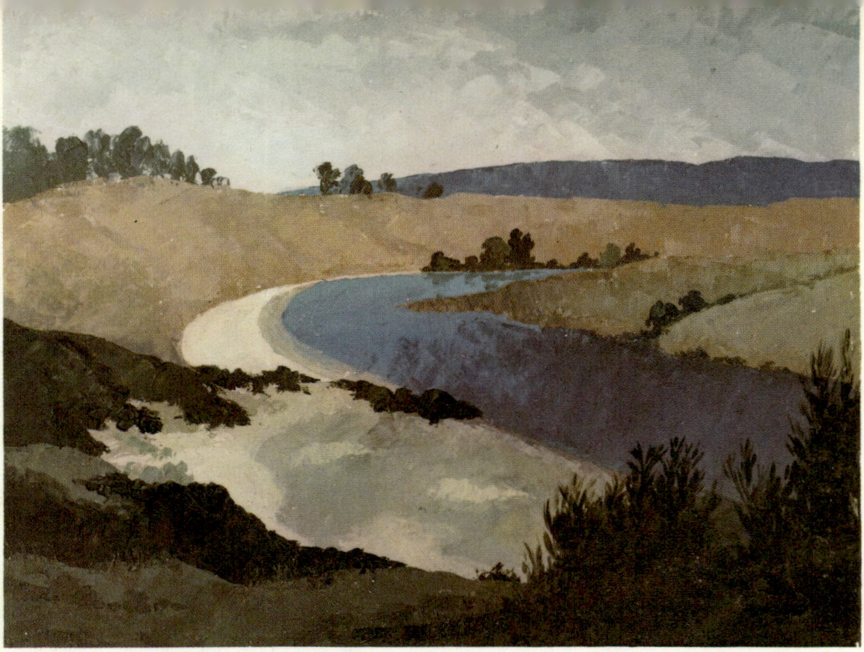

11 River Scene in Carnarvonshire, showing the sky after rain. The river featured at low tide greatly assists the curves that in turn lead to the dramatic mountains. The dark bushes in the foreground still further enhance the recession of the whole

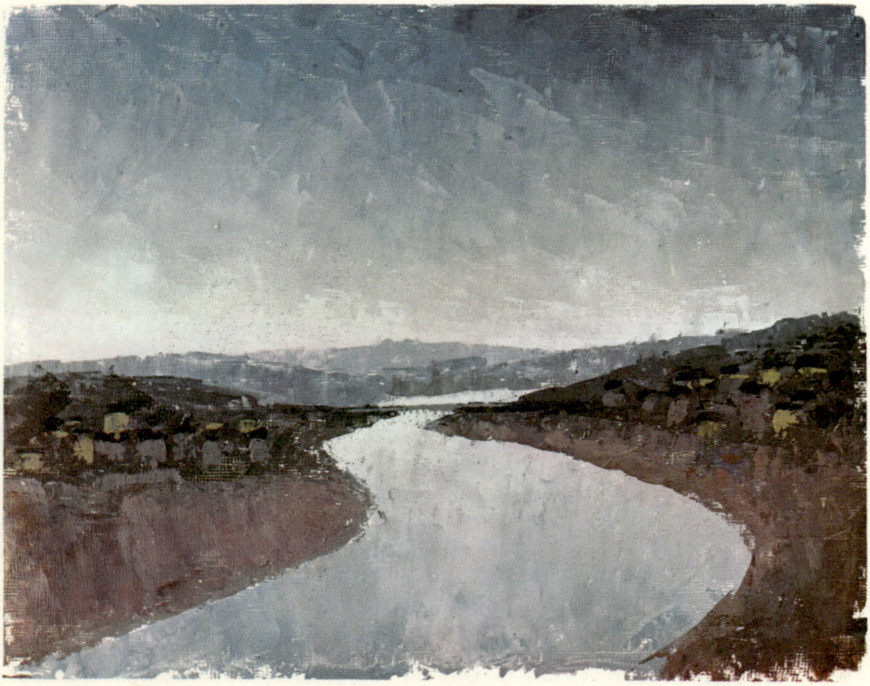

12 This sketch of the River Teign, Teignmouth, illustrates the grey light after storm. The reedy river with its graceful natural shape allows the perspective to be appreciated

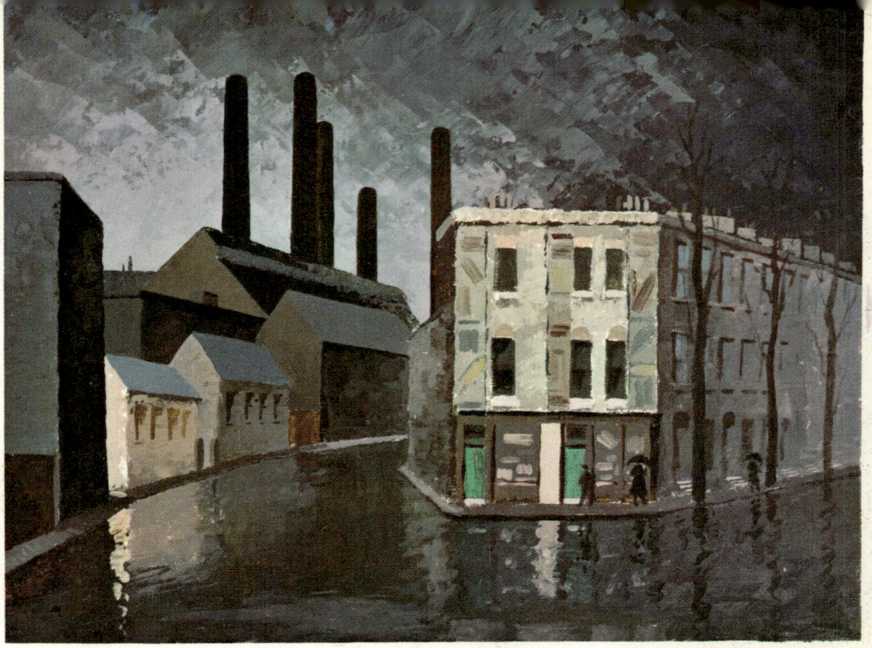

13 Lots Road, Chelsea. Sketch after a severe thunderstorm showing the dramatic light in the sky and the incidental accents of light on the buildings. These are helpful when repeated in the reflections on the wet road

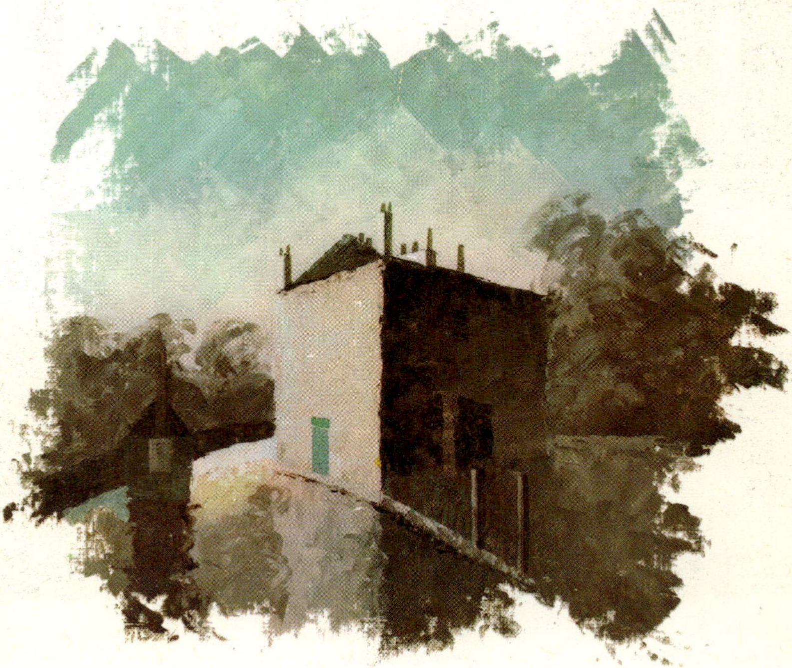

14 The Spaniard's Inn, Hampstead. The effect of the reflections in the wet road helps to complete the arrangement

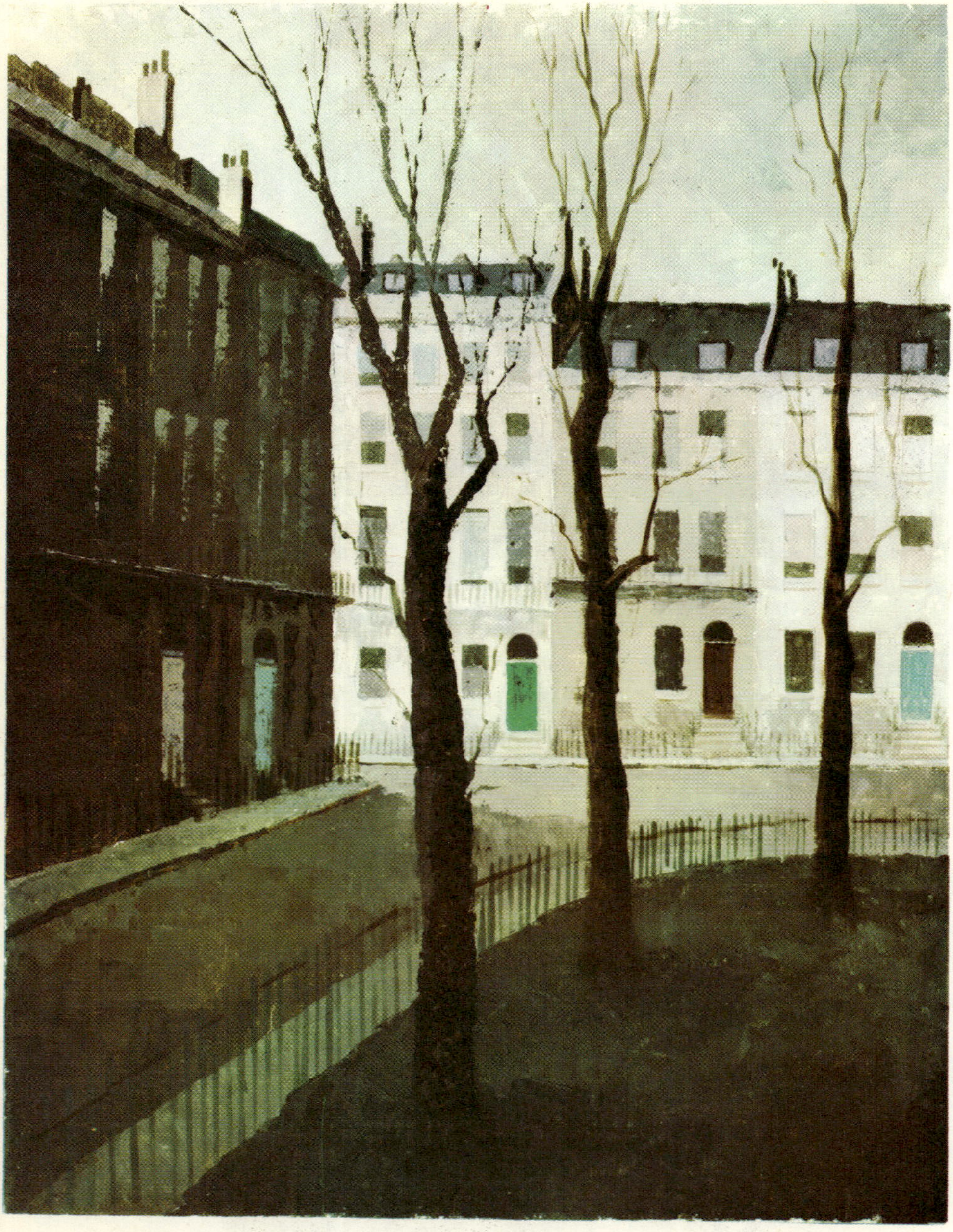

15 Bedford Square. The charm of this Georgian square is assisted by the contrasts of dark passages of the trees silhouetted against the sunlit houses. The gardens on the right assist in balancing the architecture on the left

from dull monotony. In the case of landscape we must have light, atmosphere and recession. Therefore let us first agree that the sky provides illumination to the subject. This can be a sunny day, cloudy, heavy with rain and dark storm or even a nocturne. All should produce the effect sought after. Because of this we begin by illustrating the sky, and not by painting the rest of the subject and trying to paint the sky as a sort of afterthought.

It must be understood that we begin the painting by working from the distance (the sky) to the front. Daylight subjects whether cloudy or cloudless are usually approached by putting in the sky first, and the clouds are painted in while the sky is still wet. The appearance of the sky should be even and not heavy with pigment otherwise it will present difficulties when the clouds are added.

In almost all kinds of landscape painting it has been found advisable to use the 'wet' method until the sky, clouds and distance have been completed: after this stage is finished the rest of the subject can be carried out in the ordinary way although the background is now quite dry and will remain immovable irrespective of objects painted over it.

The landscapes in Plates 8 and 9 have been completed in order that the student may appreciate the points referred to in the above chapter and be given an opportunity to study light and recession, as well as the sharper contrasts of tone values. Although simply treated, all add to the spatial quality required in a subject of this kind, thus bringing the composition to a satisfactory conclusion.

The rhythm and absence of monotony in the knife-strokes greatly assist in portraying the character of the countryside. The short upright strokes are sufficiently expressive to describe the foreground fields, whereas if the strokes had been applied horizontally they would have been less effective. This is also a good example to indicate the importance of a broad and direct approach to a subject, where the compulsory limitations of the palette knife assist in a more dramatic note as opposed to a less positive statement with brushes, which often results in what is referred to as 'knitting' when small brushes have been used.

6 GREY SUBJECTS

Within a more limited range of colour it will be found that there is a distinct harmony of tone. In each of these subjects Plates 10, 11 and 12, while the pattern changes and the details in each case are simplified and subdued, a consistency of value persists which is dominated by the influence of the low-toned sky.

The colour range of the canopy of the sky, although it is shown lighter on the horizon, is employed in all the other passages in the composition, and all the colours contain less or more derivatives of the sky colours. This explains the presence of the low-toned harmonies and the success of this type of subject which appears to be dominated by the value of the heavy brooding sky.

While the bright sunny sky will throw everything up in sharper contrasts, presenting us with gay and higher toned incidents, these three pictures depict nature in a much lower range of limited colours.

The harmony presented is best achieved by a more limited palette than would be used when painting a bright day; this would be best achieved by the use of four colours only plus white. Just as we aim for harmony and balance in our subject so we must begin by the same in our pigments. Apart from white we should provide a balance by choosing two warm colours and two

7 ARCHITECTURAL SUBJECTS

A painting devoid of good colour, interesting composition or atmosphere can be compared to a musical composition performed without expression, played or sung in dull, level tones. A painting with atmosphere possesses an instantaneous quality, conveying to the beholder a sense of intimacy which creates a feeling of unity between the artist, the picture and the spectator – which I consider often accounts for the success of many paintings. Whether the subject is selected from the ordinary things in life and their surrounding influences, or from more ambitious schemes in architecture; the work will remain less interesting and unappealing without the diffusing charm of atmosphere. Diffusion could be associated with the perspective or the introduction of the colours producing the necessary recession to be seen in the subject. The atmospheric content would be associated with the illusive mood created by associations connected with the subject.

The play of sunlight has a great attraction for many painters and so has the more subdued effect of rain with its innumerable subtleties of patches and pools of colour to be seen on wet roads.

Colour symphony is another term often used which may, to the uninitiated, provoke quite unnecessary gloom or uncertainty.

This is achieved by colour control, and colour control for any composition means only the fullest use of a limited palette; in other words, profundity from a limited range of pigments, which must inevitably bring harmony and unity of colour tones. This perplexing problem obviously cannot be dealt with to its fullest extent at this stage, but a brief excursion will surely produce some degree of profit. Much has been written and said about colour by various authorities, yet from time to time students ask most naïve questions regarding pigments; it is evident that their literal reading of what has been written has been a misinterpretation.

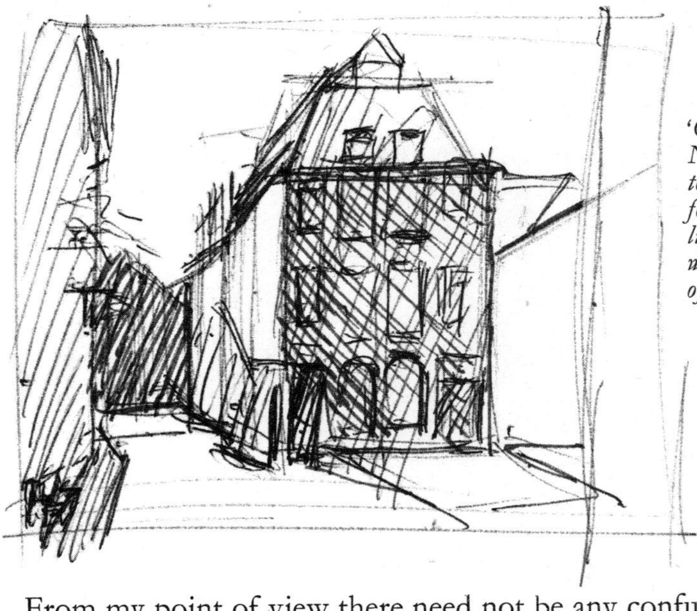

'Old Houses, Dinan, Normandy'—In addition to the historic architecture found in this city, a strong light and shade is presented which adds to the importance of the composition

From my point of view there need not be any confusion regarding colour, for whatever purpose in pictorial or commercial art it may be used, provided the artist strictly adheres to the limitation of the palette and is carried to profundity – to its fullest conclusion.

First let us contemplate any imaginary sketch or painting that is under consideration. According to the architecture or situation of the composition, this will be dominated by a certain palette. Secondly, it is of the utmost importance that the foregoing points should be conjoined with a dramatic note.

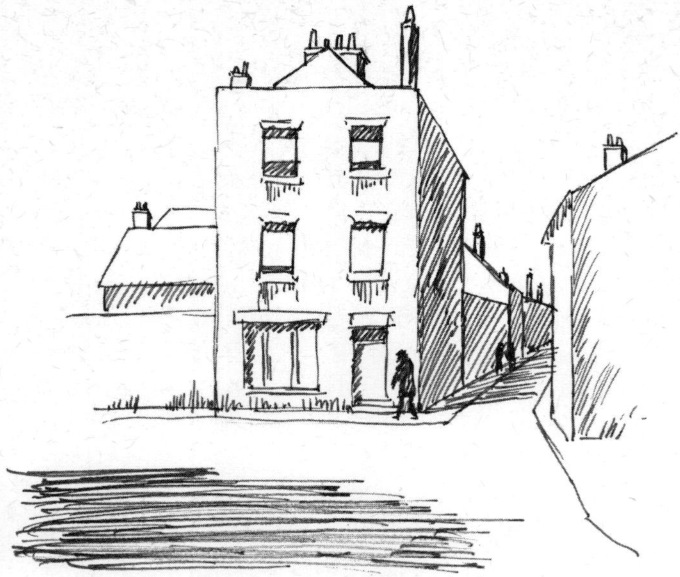

'Houses, Teignmouth, Devon'—The simplicity of the architecture is noticed in this composition. The suggestion of the foreground shadow not only balances the design, but also anchors down the drawing

Two examples of these two points will be found clearly illustrated in Plate 14, *The Spaniard's Inn, Hampstead* and Plate 15, *Bedford Square*. Both of these compositions were painted with the same two colours, Phthalo green and Burnt umber plus white, and will serve to illustrate the possibilities of the use of two colours only when they are taken to their conclusion.

The treatment of the reflections in a wet road in Plate 14 is very valuable in assisting to anchor the composition down by repeating the colours of the buildings. In the painting of *Bedford Square* the balance of tone is achieved by the heavily cast shadow in the foreground from the dark building on the left, whilst the stark trees complete a dramatic composition.

Possibly you may see a second or third dramatic note to which the eyes and mind of the viewer would first be attracted. This need not necessarily be a passage of light in the sky or on a building, but might easily be a dark building silhouetted against a storm-tossed sky. For instance in Plate 13 of *Lots Road, Chelsea*, we have a subject that in my mind epitomises all the points we have mentioned, there being a dramatic note in the violent contrast between light and the extreme depth of tone in the power station chimneys on the left. The daring introduction of the light passages and their repetition in the reflections in the wet road make the required contribution to the subject.

The palette used for this painting and also for the *Prospect of Whitby, Wapping*, were Phthalo blue, Phthalo green, Burnt umber, Yellow ochre, Cadmium red and Titanium white. These will satisfy the needs for most subjects, whether one is thinking of expression in cool or warm tones. The method of application is for most subjects somewhat immaterial, whether it be with sable brush, hog-hair brush or palette knife; the method adopted is largely dependent on the temperament of the artist or on the surface of the support he uses to paint on. It will only be after long experience that the student will realise the particular type and quality of the surface of canvas or panel most suitable to his own particular form of expression. For instance, one person may require a perfectly smooth, non-absorbent surface, while another would prefer a rougher, more absorbent surface that gives more grip or tooth, which suits his particular calligraphy. The artist

'River Teign, Teignmouth'—The acceptance of the shapes and strength of the distant hills is used to emphasise the boat houses on the left

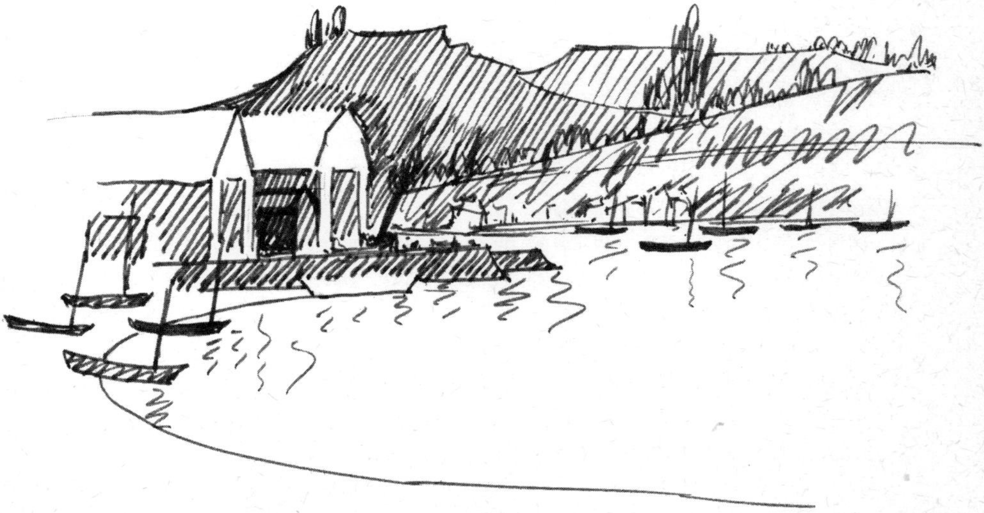

may also use different methods according to his mood and his subjects.

The colour plate of *Lots Road, Chelsea*, shows a painting carried out with both palette knife and brush – which was used for the wet road – but the illustration of *The Prospect of Whitby* was painted entirely with a palette knife. By comparison of the two plates it should be noticed that, whatever the method of expression of pigment employed, the degree of expression is not in any way impaired. The movement and fluidity, however, are the same in both methods.

It is the author's experience that some students only associate very coarse, heavy technique with palette knife painting. This need not be so. The same quality should be achieved in both methods of application. In both cases the control of the tool, whether it be bristle or steel, can come only from long experience. One should first learn to understand and appreciate the function and purpose of each. In certain architectural subjects it is an advantage to accept and to use the flexibility and awkwardness of a knife as opposed to the brush.

There is something provocative about the struggle to establish full control, to impose one's will on an instrument – in this case the knife. Such can be the artist's control that very fine lines, where the pigment is picked up from the palette in small quantities on the edge of the knife, can be applied in order to describe a broken or fine line. Quality and crispness of texture are particularly desirable in any form of painting. Disastrous results will inevitably occur if the student approaches the canvas in a negative manner, hoping for the best to happen; it seldom does – and he finds himself making mud-pies with his paint. A clear statement is more satisfactory.

It is sometimes an advantage for a student to mix various tones or tints for a passage and assemble them on the palette before applying them to the canvas. It is surely obvious that if the colours harmonise successfully and are perfectly balanced on the palette, this will be the case when they are conveyed to the canvas. This method will greatly assist in eliminating any trial by error.

Remember not to be too coarse or crude with the pigment; never try to be too careful in the preservation of the drawing already established. Quality in the painting can be achieved by the softness of edges and allowing a broken line – often described as losing and finding a line – thus producing a fluidity of texture.

Hard edges therefore should be shunned, as these contribute largely to the absence of quality in many paintings. Edges should at all times be most carefully considered. The use of the background colour or priming should be considered in relation to edges, for it is sometimes an advantage, when painting on a dark surface, to allow some of the dark background to trickle through here and there along the edges in order to achieve the broken texture and, at the same time, produce a feeling of unity. It should therefore be realised that, while the drawing should be accurate, some of this is lost in the painting in order to replace accuracy with subtlety.

In the illustration of *Lots Road, Chelsea*, a wet day is depicted. Here particularly the subtlety and softness of line makes a great contribution to the wet atmospheric effect. It should also be noticed that on a wet, dull day the sharp definition of tone between the areas of colour on the light side is in far less contrast to the dark side than would be the case on a brighter day.

While the choice of subject is important to sustain the interest and excitement of the student, the arrangement of the composition is of equal importance.

One cannot always place on record everything which might come within the picture plane of one's view. The balance of a shape of light and dark passages of buildings should be so arranged as to produce a central note of interest. This then is to be reinforced by what is decided on as the dramatic note to develop the interest after the eye of the viewer has been brought to the focal point.

For the same reason and purpose, groups of figures will often provide the necessary contrast of tone value and give movement to the subject. It should not be overlooked that lamp-posts are

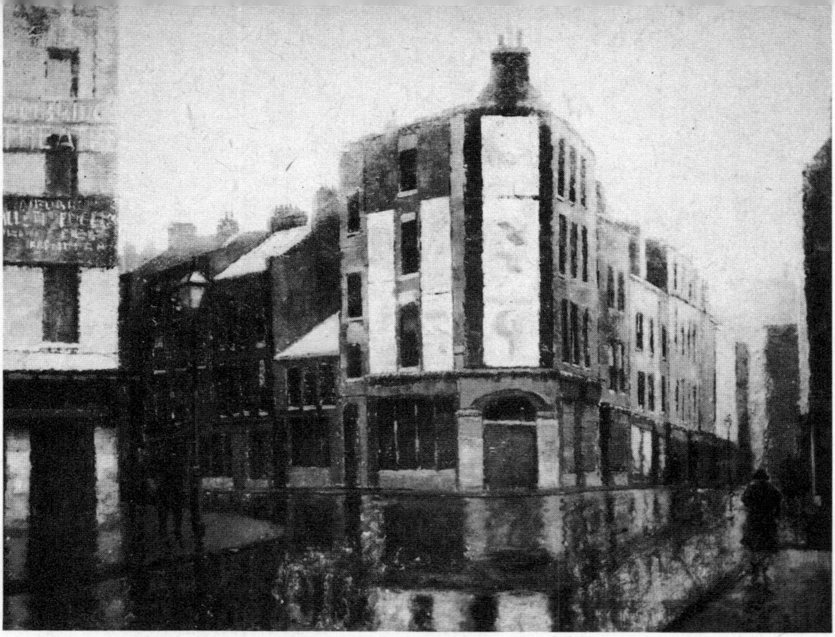

'Seven Dials, W.C.1'—The reflections which repeat the colours – in a lower tone – of the buildings balance the composition

sometimes moved without the permission of the borough surveyor in order to restore a balance of tone!

Very often one is asked by students, 'Do you paint your pictures out of doors or in the studio?' This is a very interesting question, but the correct answer is 'Both'. For instance, one goes out of doors to sketch or merely to make notes in order to build up a larger composition which obviously could not be done out of doors. For this purpose Polymer colours are ideally suitable because they dry quickly for transporting back to the studio. These outdoor sketches are often in great demand because they possess a charm in their spontaneous expression which is sometimes difficult to achieve when the artist is considering more logically a larger and more ambitious subject. The spirit and composition of the sketch must, of necessity, be simpler both in drawing and in arrangement, and an endeavour should be made to finish a small sketch of this nature in one sitting of not more than two-and-a-half hours. It should be obvious that, if the subject is continued beyond this time, the light will have changed and neutralised the very essence of the scene's first appeal.

8 CORRECT TONE AND UNITY

Although the title of this book is mainly concerned with Polymer and its many uses, we should include a description of correct tone which is of great importance whatever the pigment or whatever the subject may be.

An artist's perception of his subject, no matter what the composition may be, should always be expressed in his own personal style which is part of his technique and reaction to colour, but success can only be achieved when there is correct tone present in the subject.

Generally speaking students think only of tone in relation to tonal or low-toned paintings. But on a closer investigation it is evident that this subject embraces almost every form of painting which is accepted as good, either for its colour or its tone values. Where rhythm and tone value, whether of balance or of light, are present, one must agree that the painting has good tonal qualities, so naturally a painting where there is an absence of these qualities must possess incorrect tone.

To achieve success with a painting by ensuring good tone it is essential to have a limited or controlled palette, thus making it easier to reach the desired unity of colour. Therefore, having selected your colours for a subject, any deviation from this by the introduction of another colour, other than those chosen, to be used solely for one note or passage would create incorrect tone. For instance, the colour plate 13, *Lots Road*, *Chelsea*, shows a street with a grey sky after rain has ceased and the buildings and the road are influenced by the colour of the sky. This produces tonal quality. But if one can visualise the effect of the same scene painted exactly as it is but with a bright blue sky it would be an example of incorrect tone. Alternatively if the sky had been blue the influence of that particular colour would have predominated, and blue would have shown its influence on the whole of the tonal qualities of the painting.

This same rule applies whether it is a landscape, still-life, marine or even portraiture. It is just this knowledge of light unity which helps to produce the harmony or contrasts necessary for good tone, which includes good colour.

Unity, or 'knitting together' of one's colour scheme, can often be assisted by the choice of the right tone or priming of a canvas. Rembrandt throughout his life experimented with warm and cool backgrounds and in this way he allowed the colour of his background to trickle through his paint in so charming a manner that it became part of the painting itself, achieving a unity of colour and tone which we have all come to admire.

One can see, by comparison with the works of some contemporary painters, how the great masters achieved the success they deserved. Tone is a subject which always perplexes the beginner in art. The professional, by a long training in observation, has learnt to recognise the influence that unity has on the subject. This may be the prevailing light or the toned ground but both will help the saturation.

For those who embark on portraiture, the same rule applies to a large extent. A unity of background tone and figure is essential. Any deviation from this will produce incorrect tone as one is influenced by the other. Whatever the colour of the background may be, reflective colours either on the drapery, hair or on the flesh will be found to be derivative, thus assisting the tonal unity. Another good plan, and one often employed by the professional portrait painter, is to introduce some of the colours used in the portrait into the background.

9 *PICTORIAL PERSPECTIVE*

Although a profound knowledge of perspective is not always necessary for the painter, sometimes a pleasant subject can be disturbing where the student has ignored the elementary rules of perspective. The offending detail where the drawing has been allowed to get out of hand would be immediately pounced upon by the viewer. One must remember that an experienced eye will see a mistake in drawing before looking at any other quality the painting may possess.

When one has paid so much attention to such things as colour, composition, technique and unity, it would surely be unfortunate if a mistake in drawing should occur, as errors of this kind should not be made. This need not happen if one is taught to understand the simple rules of this subject. Apart from an architectural or geometric approach, which is too complicated for the artist, the understanding and application of pictorial perspective is a much simpler version which everyone should be able to understand. Naturally this subject applies mostly to buildings, interiors or exteriors and such details as figures and lamp-posts, and less so to landscape, although some awareness of recession is always shown but not as obviously as with architecture.

Firstly we must continue our powers of observation by looking at the size of any objects around us. For instance doorways vary considerably in size according to the type of building, a small cottage doorway is probably about six feet six inches whilst the entrance to a large building may even be twelve feet high. Windows are usually in proportion to the scale of the building with the upper windows smaller than the lower ones. Lamp-posts vary in height, but let us say that the older type are about thirteen feet high which gives us a chance to see the height of a person of say five foot six inches against it. As well as a doorway, this gives us a comparative size of our requirements for a street scene. We must however always be observant of everything around us – by noting the size of a taxi-cab against the lamp or the height of a figure as he stands beside the cab, the size of a bus in relation to another object or people striding on to a bus. All this is part of our comparative observation which is required when scenes are placed in perspective, for just as the buildings become smaller as they go into the distance so correspondingly do other objects. The scale of the buildings remains the same wherever they are and so does everything else.

To apply these gleanings of knowledge from our observation and introduce them into our drawing let us understand that there must always be an imaginary line drawn across the picture which we will call the eye-level – note the line across the subject in Plate 17 which represents the eye-level. This is referred to by

'Trees in Perspective'—Shown by the varied values of tones. The upright dark trees on the left add to the general effect besides stopping the design running out of the picture

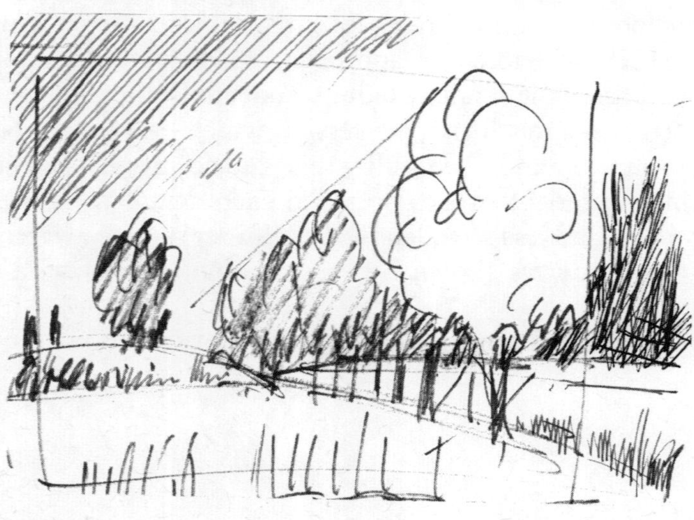

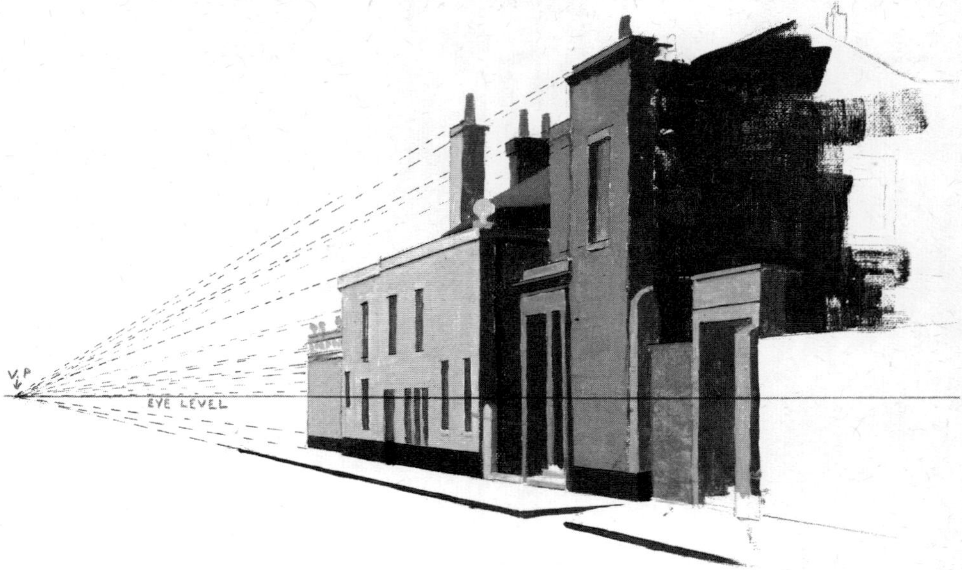

'Chelsea Arts Club'

different names such as the 'line of heights' or the 'horizon line', but let us understand it for the sake of consistency as the 'eye-level' which will always be found horizontal across the subject. The position of this line can be imagined at almost any height according to where the viewer is standing. For instance if one is standing in the road the line will be level with the viewer's height. If on the other hand one is looking from an elevated position such as an upper window, the eye-level will be correspondingly high if the line is drawn to represent an horizon when the viewer is looking straight ahead and not looking downwards.

This then is the eye-level and it is on this line that there will be found the vanishing point, according to the subject. Sometimes there may be more than one point as another vanishing point would be required for the receding lines of buildings on the other side of the road. But whichever part of the composition is being drawn all the lines should be shown receding to their own respective vanishing point.

Remember that all lines below the eye-level run upwards to their vanishing point and lines above run downwards. The sketch of the *Chelsea Arts Club* clearly shows the direction of all these lines.

10 BOATS AND HARBOURS

It is generally understood that Van Gogh allowed himself to be thoroughly absorbed in his subject whilst painting it in order to reproduce the atmospheric impact that the composition had upon him. It is known that in order to paint sunshine and register the fierceness of its rays he would paint for hours without protection, thus increasing his susceptibility to sunstroke. Likewise he would go out in the heavy rain, getting soaking wet in the process, in order to depict a storm.

Whether your subject is concerned with the ordinary things of life and their surroundings – such as a very simple arrangement of objects to be seen in anyone's kitchen – or a more ambitious composition, either indoors or outdoors, the work will remain ordinary and pedestrian without the subtle and diffusing charm of atmosphere. This rather illusive term could be used to describe the activity of the subject or its stillness and the tranquillity which in turn produce the artist's reaction and expression.

Apart from a professional ability to draw and paint anything, there is no need to join the Merchant Navy to draw and paint ships, neither do you have to become a horticulturist before you can paint flowers! Our training in observation will give us the necessary 'know-how' about ships and boats and too much knowledge of marine architecture would destroy our own personal reaction.

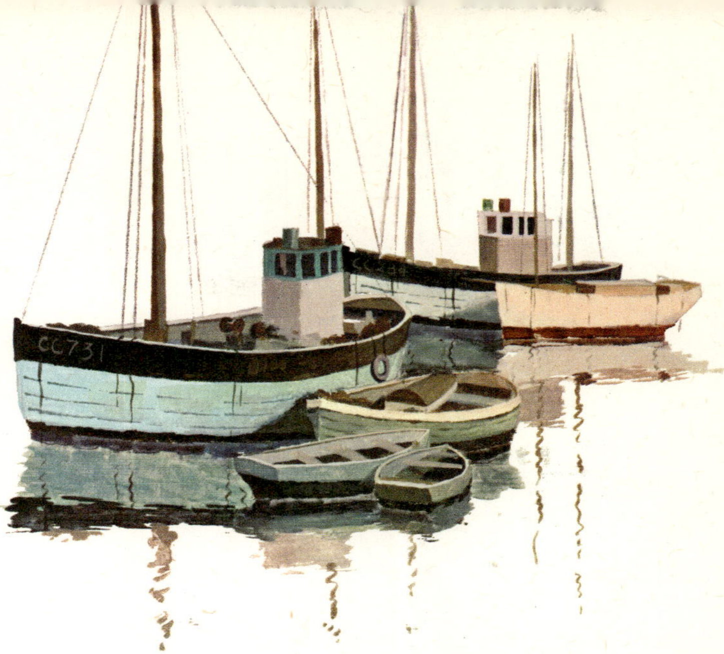

16 Detail of Fishing Boats. This drawing is of commercial craft which figure mainly in the harbour in Concarneau, Brittany. The colourful boats and sails reflected in the still waters make a very happy painting of a marine subject

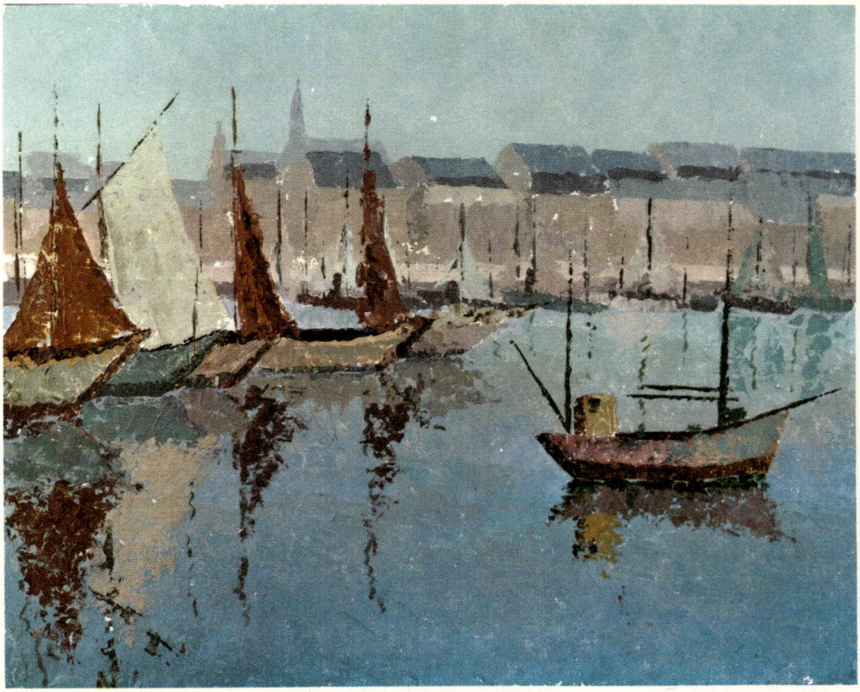

17 The Harbour, Concarneau. This shows the buildings beside the harbour which help to separate the sky from the subject and also add some recession to the composition. The fishing boat anchored on the right restores the balance of shapes in the displacement of the craft

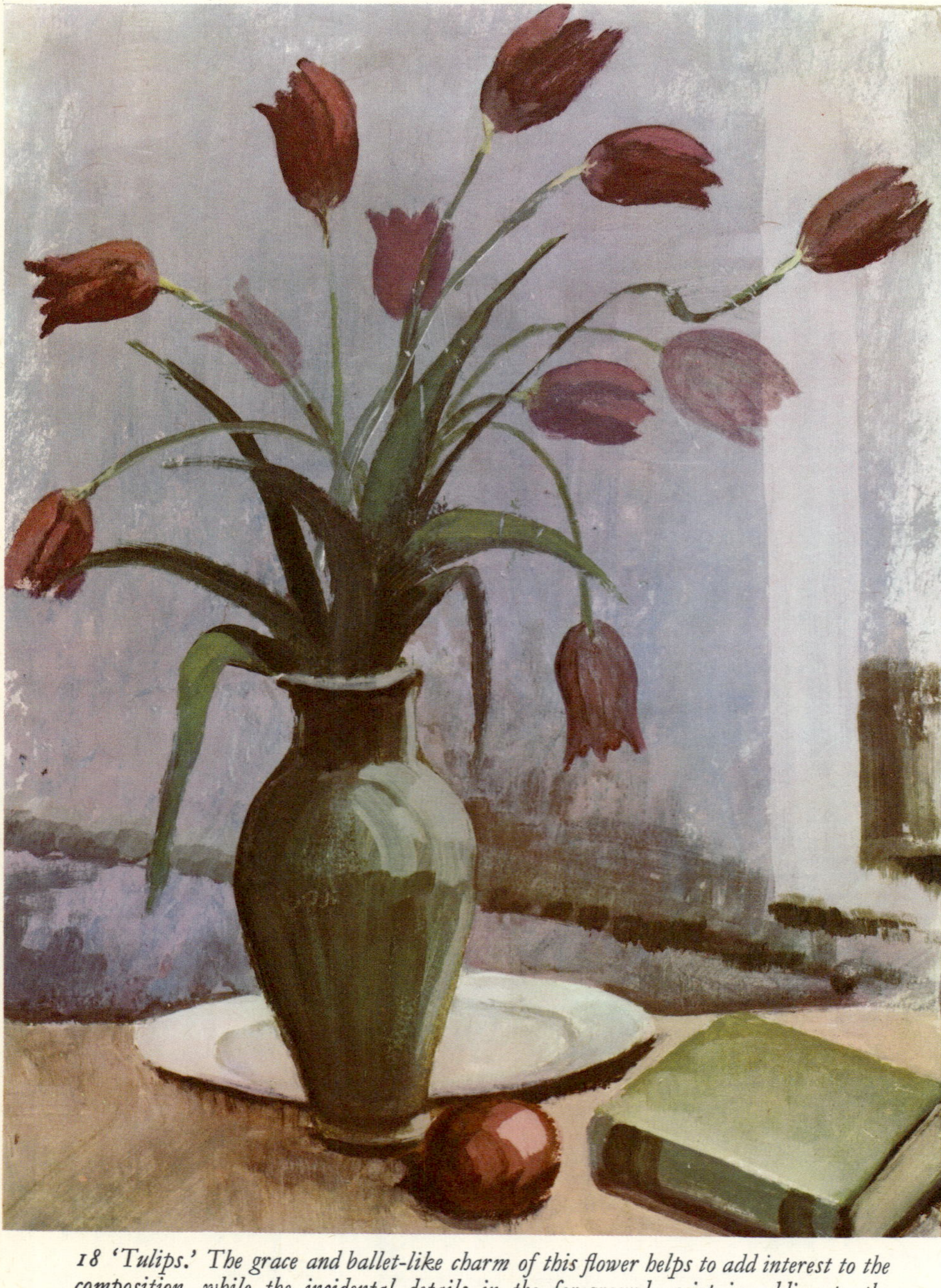

18 'Tulips.' The grace and ballet-like charm of this flower helps to add interest to the composition, while the incidental details in the foreground assist in adding to the arrangement

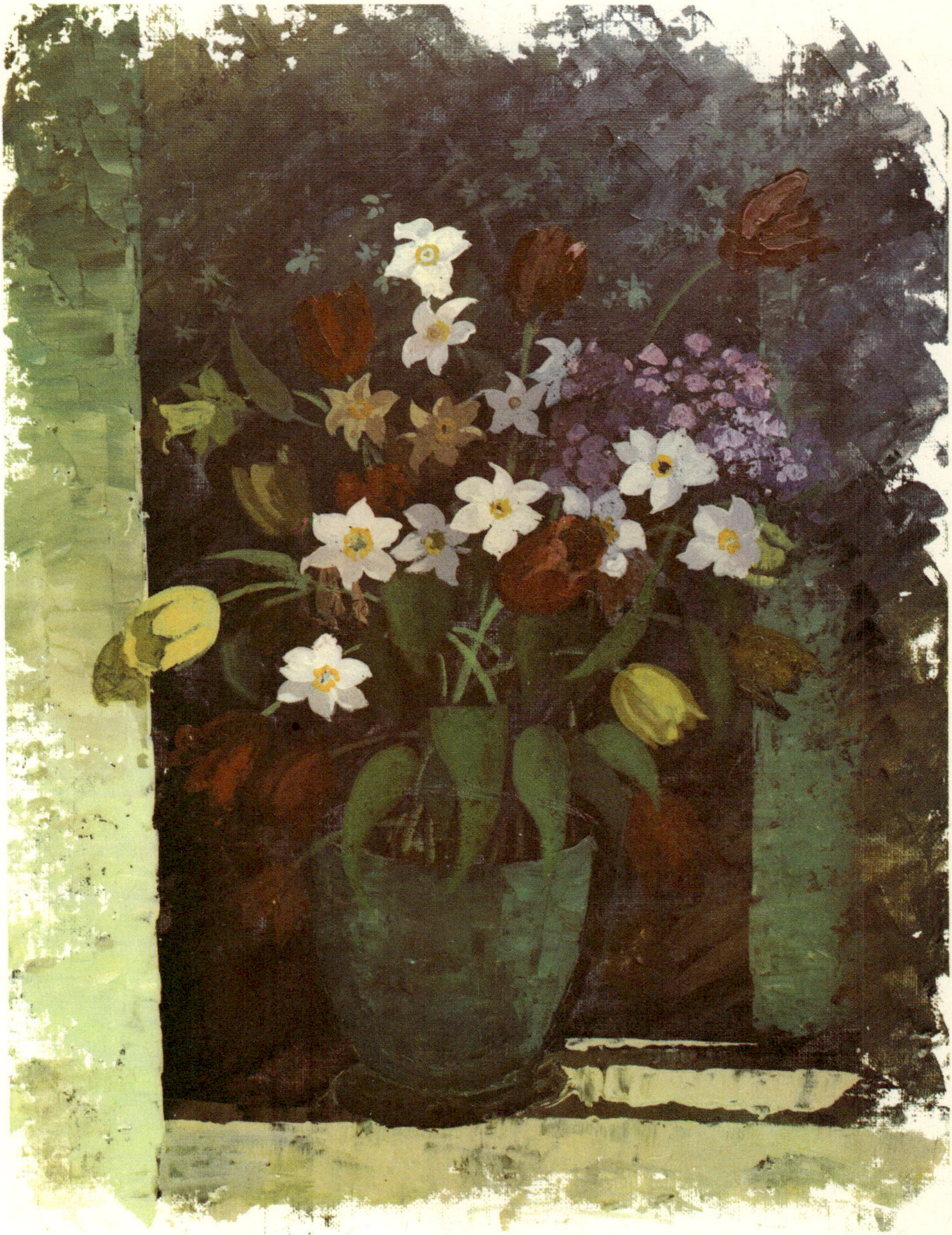

19 Profusion in a Mixed Group. The details found in the various flowers were introduced with a soft brush and a knife was used for the broader passages in the foreground. The perspective was introduced with the softer treatment of the distant flowers, often described as the semi-throwing-away treatment

cool colours and these would be obtained by Blue, Umber, Yellow ochre and Indian red. Generally this is the basis but the variations are numerous owing to the colours available. The sky was painted in the same way as described in Chapter 4 'Skies and Landscapes', and, as before, it was carried out with a palette knife with the same facility as already shown in previous plates.

Frequently one hears a student remark that the colour of the water is always changing. This is always because the elements and the sky are different. Seldom are they always constant, but if we remember the cause of the changes and adhere to our original colour scheme we should achieve the desired harmony.

'Twilight'—The dramatic effect of the grey evening is highlighted by the receding perspective of the road pavement and river which focus the evening light

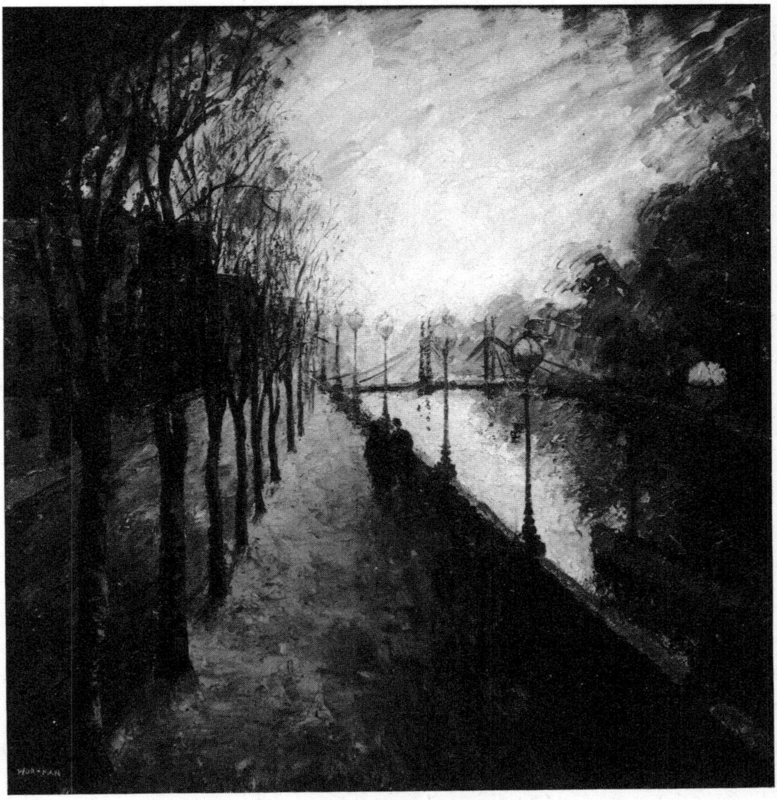

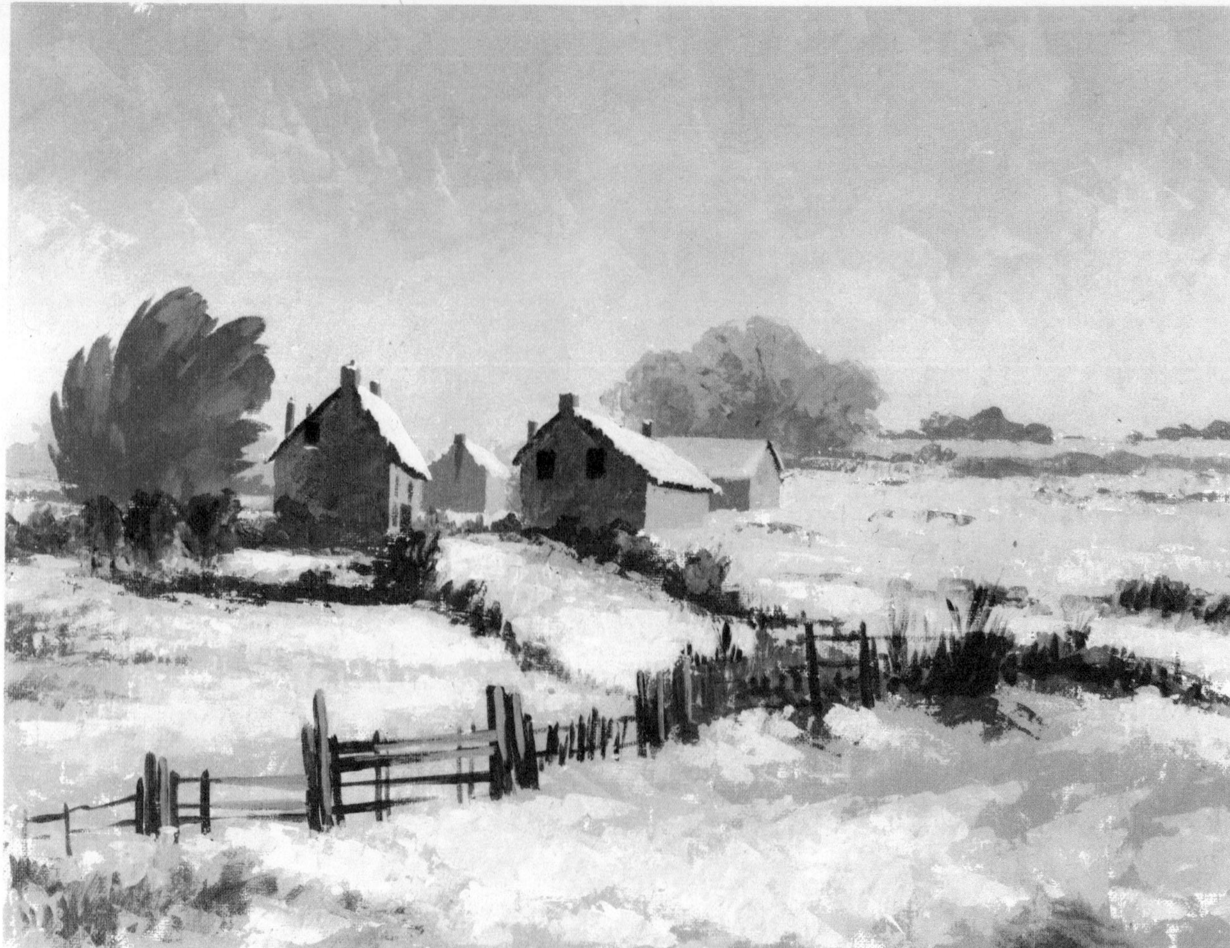

20 Snow Scene. The subtlety of a snow scene can be seen when contrasted against the snow-laden sky. The various colours will be found to be derivatives from buildings and trees, thus helping to unify the sky and the snow-covered ground

The atmosphere we seek to express depends considerably on the capture of the moment of impact, and yet contains much that is visible in the subject. For instance, in the painting of *The Harbour, Concarneau*, I had to penetrate beyond the ordinary visibility and aspects of the commonplace to create the feeling and expression of this sunlit harbour with its accompanying emotional effects of the various crafts in their gay colours and all casting their own dancing reflections in the hazy heat of the moment (Plate 17).

I have studied boats of most kinds and in all seasons and proved that as a result of the different elements present at the time when the colour, movement and reflections are affected, a feeling of rhythm is produced – always in tune with the particular mood presented. Therefore to attain the correct atmosphere, the student must see he paints the rhythm produced, making sure that all in the painting contributes to the whole rhythmic unity of the composition: light, subject, colour, harmony, emotion and familiar characteristics combining towards correct atmosphere which will either make or mar the picture.

Although the subject of *Concarneau* is painted in a virile style, it has plastic qualities due to the use of the Polymer pigment, particularly noted in the masts, sails and reflections in the water, bringing together the atmosphere of the sky and sea creating an almost imperceptible veil over the whole subject and producing the required unity that a harbour scene of this type can create. In this painting the ground on the canvas was treated with a light colour and a great deal of this was allowed to trickle through the edges of the paint, which assisted in producing the veiled effect of the composition. It is important for the student to decide what is the characteristic mood he desires to convey, whether it is a summer day or an overcast stormy day; both can be helped by the right colour of the ground used. A composition of the industrious activity of a group of fishing boats, with the intricacies of the details used in their particular search of the sea, is always interesting. This requires a slightly different manner of approach to express the many cadences that combine to produce the relative atmosphere of the chosen subject, and one must

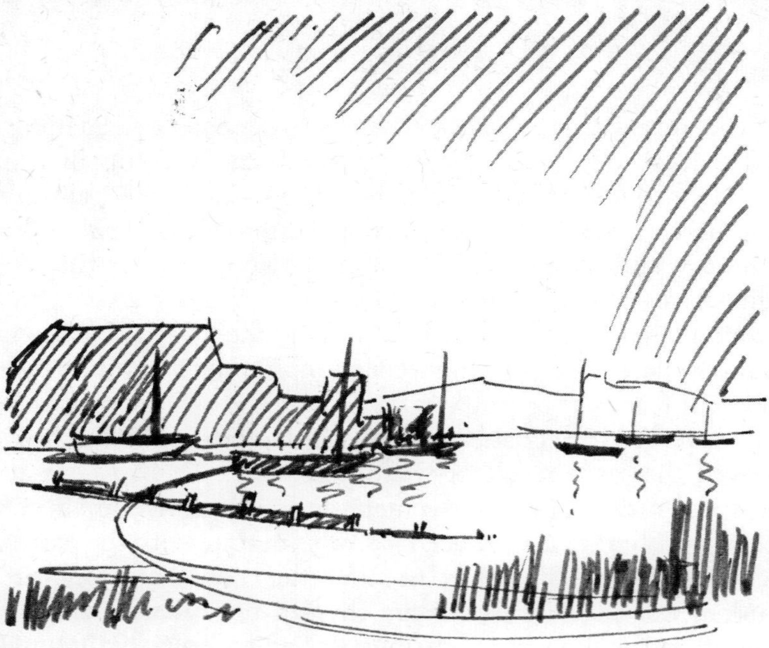

The massed details in this sketch in the left middle distance are complemented by the shadow in the sky which radiates towards the focal point of the picture and is balanced by the dark outline of reeds in the foreground

learn to be adjusted mentally as quickly as possible and artistically detach oneself from any disturbing surroundings. Thus the artist will be able to catch the appropriate atmosphere and ultimately convey the scene to canvas.

The artist must not become confused and think he must present the subject as a mirror reflecting every detail – he must remember to mould or paint what he observes to his will and manifest his work in its own essence.

As will be appreciated, a composition of this kind presented many difficulties before a satisfactory arrangement could be arrived at. The first visit to the harbour with its throb of life, the smell of fishing boats, the loading and unloading of fish and ice, left one with a feeling of bewilderment. It was not possible at first to obtain a clear idea of the kind of composition which would embrace all the aspects of this fishing harbour; this was decided later after a careful study of the many drawings and colour sketches that were made. This enabled me to begin the actual painting using a direct method where the right colour was applied first time to obviate any alterations. In this case I began with the sky and worked towards the front, dropping in the reflections on to the wet painted water. Admittedly one must not only be sure of one's colour but also of oneself before one begins direct painting of this kind and in this manner.

The sketch of fishing boats in Plate 16 is one of the many studies made of craft to be seen in a harbour. There is a fascination attached to fishing craft, not only in colour and shape, but also of the spirit of adventure usually associated with those who sail the seas in order to earn a livelihood. All weathers have to be faced to bring food to our table. Sometimes the sea is rough, accompanied by strong gales, but whatever the weather these brave seamen sail out from their quiet protected harbours to haul fish for our benefit. The fishing boats that they sail in vary according to their home port or their country of origin. All these details will be noted in a general study of this type of craft; a distinct difference will be noticed between a type of boat used in the Orkneys compared with a Brixham trawler. The colours used by the seamen are variable too. For instance the fishermen in Brittany will employ the gayest of colours for their craft and

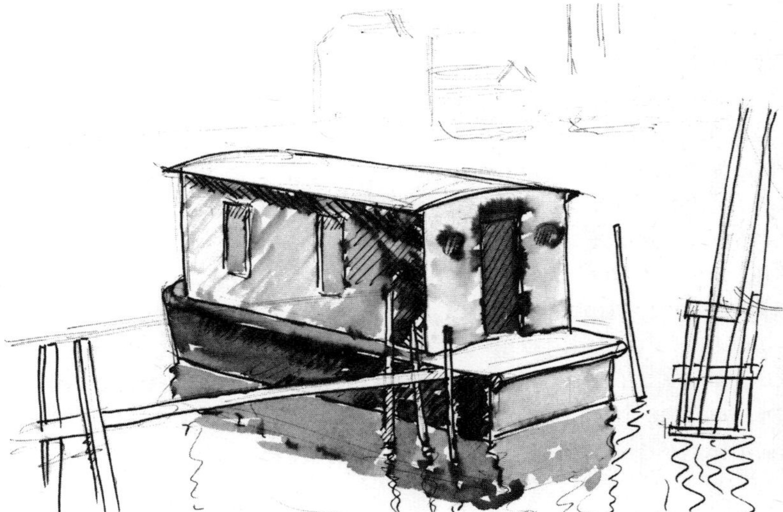

choose bright-coloured fabrics for the sails, whilst the boats in England will often be painted black or brown unless they are private sailing craft, when they are usually painted brighter.

The tackle and ropes are usually the same and one will notice the ends of ropes dangling over the sides which must be included as they help to make the boat appear to be lived in or in use. The heights of the masts vary as do also the pulleys. The sardine or tunny boats in *Concarneau* usually have tall masts to carry more sail.

When arranging the composition, a generally accepted rule is that a horizontal line half-way across the canvas should be avoided as this would produce the effect of cutting the picture in two equal halves and would be detrimental to a good composition. The introduction of buildings, often to be seen alongside most harbours, helps us to introduce a broken sky-line which is helpful in many subjects besides making an interesting background to the gaily painted boats in the harbour. Even if there is a mist present to soften the buildings it gives the artist an opportunity to introduce an interesting subtlety which is often lacking on a sunlit day.

Rarely out of doors can one find an almost perfect subject awaiting the artist to give his interpretation; only a few alterations were required to make the composition complete to my satisfaction. Most of the picture was painted direct from nature where the sky and the light presented a rich-toned subject worthy of any marine painter. An amateur painter sometimes fails to visualise the impact of a subject. The potentialities of the boats in the reduced light and in their naturalistic setting could not be overlooked.

The area of the sky is small and of secondary importance. It was therefore reduced in tone value to the general surroundings so that the blue hills conveyed their message with clarity, thus linking up with the colour of the river and the insistence of the shapes of the boats on the beach, where it was preferable to stress the rigid shapes rather than make a timid approach.

11 PAINTING FLOWER SUBJECTS

In describing the painting of different flower subjects in various mediums, I find that the best results are obtained with an opaque pigment such as Polymer. Ordinary watercolours require a great deal more control and discipline which can easily go wrong when painting flowers. In this new pigment, however, because it is quick drying and will not lift when a succeeding coat of paint is added or changes are made during any alterations of design, I find it most suitable for this type of work.

When arranging the blooms, do not just bunch them into a large lump and force them into a jar; think of them as something delicate and fragile whose living force pours out colour and beauty for your temporary enjoyment. We are trying to capture and record our reactions to the beauty and fragrance before us. We must think of the flower arrangement as the blooms affect us and the creative moods they inspire, so let them have some space to express their design, even the length of the stalk and leaves have something to say, when you allow them to say it. This is particularly noticeable with tulips and daffodils, which have the charm of a ballet dancer. The smaller flowers and many of the short-stemmed type can often be arranged suitably in a 'mixed bunch' but not to overcrowd the display.

Always avoid artificial flowers when fresh ones are available.

No matter what you pay for the manufactured article, the result will always look lifeless and lacking in the living force of the natural flower. After all it is the aura of life, fugitive though it may be, which is largely responsible for our inspiration and creation of the subject. This then will help us to keep in tune with our model and assist us in arriving at the harmony and perfection we seek to achieve. Much of the satisfaction in painting of this kind is in adjusting one's wavelength to the subject and in making one's own discoveries, either in an expression with a brush or indeed with a palette knife. Apart from the approach one would use in the painting of a mural in its flat pattern, certain fundamentals must be expressed. Therefore one's attitude of mind in the making of a picture is important before what is observed can be fully expressed. There must be a oneness of the composition, harmony and good colour either in rich high tones or a satisfying lower keyed octave. It is an expression that tests all the artist's mental and emotional qualities in order to adjust his own technical expression to the subject. Everyone has a different technique which runs through all his work: it is like the calligraphy in handwriting; it is part of the personality of the painter.

Most people, however, prefer to use a brush to express the form of leaves and petals, but whatever type of tool is used the object must be the same and reach the same satisfactory conclusion.

In Plate 18 where a study of tulips has been used a small range of colours has been employed to achieve a low-toned harmony. The colours were Alizarin crimson, Phthalo green, Ultramarine, Yellow ochre and Burnt umber plus Titanium white. The distant flowers were treated with less insistence than the foreground ones which were dropped in while the background was still wet, thus assisting the illusion of space and recession which should always be noted. The other shapes on the table were included in order to anchor down the composition and the colour scheme.

Profusion in a Mixed Group, in Plate 19, has two other colours added, which were Cadmium red and Cadmium yellow. These were necessary to lift up the key as well as illustrating the varied flowers. The dark background was painted first, using derivatives of the colours to be employed for the blooms, but without using any white except for the sides and the base where a little white was added where required. The next to be painted were the flowers vaguely to be seen in the background. The leaves and stalks were next, taking a careful note of the changing values of the greens – dark ones and light ones – and finally the nearer blooms were added which completed a feeling of space and recession.

Flowers should not be painted flat as though they had been pressed into a book, but in different shapes and positions, some hanging down or showing a side view as well as the different tones or colours as they are affected by the light or the spatial position. All these details should be considered to assist in a satisfactory presentation.

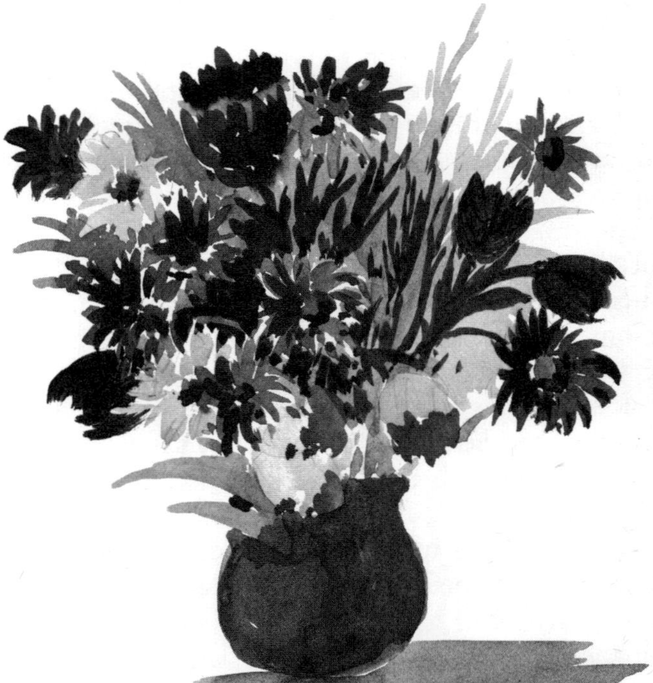

12 | *ON SNOW SCENES*

Although many artists, at different times of their career, succumb to the charm of landscape covered in snow, out of the hundreds painted possibly not more than ten per cent fully succeed in achieving the true tone and colour value of snow in winter.

Just as any subject at different times of the day or in any season is, in every case, influenced by the particular type of light present at the time, so it is with the subject covered in snow. Having reached an understanding on this point let us also appreciate that skies in winter vary just as much as at any other time of the year. The sky could be bright blue and having a wisp of cloud as is to be found in Norway, where great luminosity of light from the spectrum is seen in the apparent white snow. The colour value of these northern winters is not achieved by white paint alone but by the full use of colour found in the palest derivatives from the origin of light which is the spectrum. This is after all the snow has fallen on the landscape and is illuminated by the clear sky.

Farther south, and in England particularly, we notice a very heavy sky – either before or after the snow has fallen – which could vary in colour according to the amount of snow still in the air and, lit up behind by bright sunshine, will sometimes produce a rich pink glow which acts as a prism and diffuses the spectrum as seen in Plate 20. This then is the diffused light to which all our colours reflected in the scene owe their origin. The absence of pure white pigment produces more luminosity when these are of the value of 'mother of pearl', either the values to be found on the light side or those on the shade side. White paint alone is a dead colour and has no vibrations but it should be tinted to become very pale cream, pink, green, blue or mauve; thus infusing light into the subject and producing a thrill of excitement which can be analysed in most snow scenes.

The great masters in painting who have preceded us, and who always observed nature with great humility, expressed it through eyes which had spent many years in observing and perfecting what they could see. Painting was to them the basis for accepting a complete understanding of colour and composition.

Unfortunately a student sometimes tries a short cut, thus eliminating certain very necessary hours of observation. He has probably learned that he can produce a 'modern' work without having studied and made sketches of his subject from nature, without which any success he enjoys will be temporary. It is surely not difficult to appreciate what could happen if a singer or pianist were to give a public recital without having previously studied and mastered his expression.

I would like to reiterate that there is no easy or quick way to fame. Everyone will stumble across technical or artistic difficulties, but all can be overcome with constant study and observation.

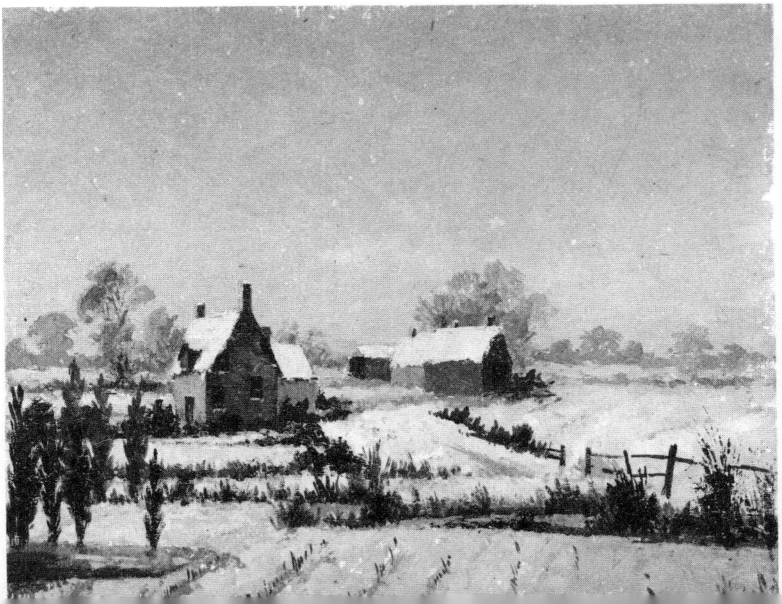

'Winter landscape'

13 AN ANALYSIS OF ABSTRACT PAINTING

Such terms as Metaphysical Aesthetics, Pop Art, Constructivism or in fact any other psychology of art owe their origin to abstract or a category which was once related to some kind of objective art. Like all metaphysical imagination of form, colour or composition, where they have strayed too far from the objectivity seen in the work they began with, they rarely reach beyond the point of a popular romanticism, fashionable though it may be to a very small circle. Metaphysical aesthetics is usually discussed in relation to some categories of abstract art but because of the introduction of the strangest ideas of form is seldom related to figurative or objective painting. However, in this chapter we hope to confine our discussion to pure abstraction from a recognisable source and not a figment of thought which has long since ceased to have an association with its source.

The student today finds himself confronted with so many tendencies and expressions that it becomes increasingly difficult for him to concentrate and steer towards a satisfying career. Still, there are many branches of art to choose from and he is less liable to suffocation – as would be the position were there to be only one school of painting with no choice left to him to satisfy his craving for expression.

Some feel that abstract art is the progressive art of today. It seems to me that there are too many branches and offshoots from the abstract movement though each has a limited number of followers; it has, in fact, too many adepts who strive to be noticed, either by the subject or the frameless size of the work. If only they realised that this completely unreadable work keeps them in a definitely illusionary *avant-garde* position while the more sensitive and original progressive continues to prosper artistically.

For nearly fifty years these *avant-garde* artists have entered into many different experiments, either in so-called sculpture, painting or oddly shaped wooden constructions. Obviously some of these experiments will remain to take their place in the history of art where all experiments are recorded to illustrate to future historians the complexes of our age. Everything in our age is noted and is definitely not unrelated to all the happenings on our planet.

Let us therefore return to nature, though we may be concerned with an abstraction from it, where we cannot go far wrong in returning to our human origin. Nature is beautifully rich and has never been fully expressed from its many angles and incidents, though artists throughout the ages, who have often never met, have expressed the most original themes through their own genius and temperament where they attained dizzy heights of expression for our admiration.

In his work, every artist depicts a new expression of his subject due to the particular impact he has received from it. Frequently an ordinary object instantly becomes something of joy because of the visual interpretation by the artist. This difference in expression is interwoven and part of the psychological build-up of the painter.

Any student should accept the urge to express and paint his impressions and ideas; although some of these occasions may be purely decorative or pictorial, they will be a record of his environment. In due course he will realise his limitations, his awakening will develop his critical sense and with it the need for a still greater understanding and a desire for more subtle statement. The joy of painting and to give expression in terms of different shapes and colour the various scenes and objects which he had failed to notice before – the colour of those buildings against the sky or the changing values in the hills and landscape – all help him to discover the beauty of things around him.

Any artist, whoever he may be, does not reproduce nature as it is; he moulds it to his personal vision and invariably simplifies to create a further impact and dissipate any unwanted detail.

A particularly good example of this simplification and reducing of detail is in Plates 21 and 22 of *The Thames*, *London Bridge*, where, apart from colour, the mere framework of the composition has been used without eliminating any of its architectural significance such as the dome of St Paul's and the Monument.

Without losing any historical features and still creating a further impact I found the only way was to take an abstraction from it and concentrate on the noticeable details. By enlarging the part of the design that I found of most interest, I treated this boldly using a large flat sable brush, preserving as much of the white canvas as possible. This simple statement can be termed a semi-abstract and possesses a great deal more emotional impact than the more literal or topographical expression.

The subject in Plate 24, *Landscape in Kent*, was painted entirely with a palette knife and again including only a limited amount of detail. The composition was painted and selected with the purpose of creating an abstract from it. All subjects are not always suitable for this type of expression. In this case several attempts at abstraction were done before a suitable arrangement was found to be satisfactory. Very little association with the original was found to have been included in this abstract. The employment of a large brush enabled my response to the particular mood required to express the perpendicular and horizontal calligraphy. This I found conveyed everything I felt was needed to produce this exciting abstract which clearly illustrates the possibilities of the right subject.

The Polymer paint was thinned with water and the brush was fully charged with the colour so that each stroke was expressed first time.

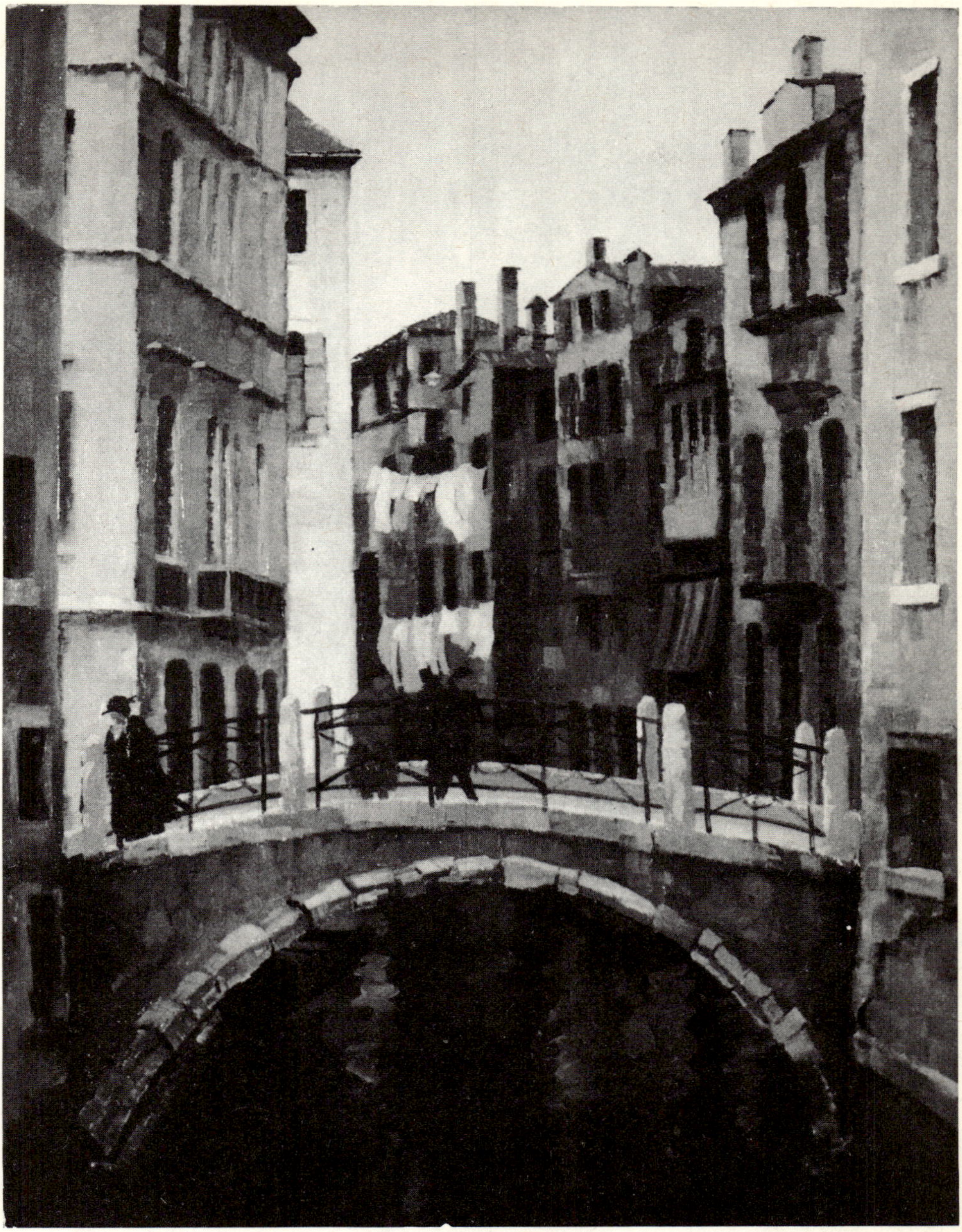

'Ponte Dei Fasere, Venice'—This is typical of one of about 200 canals in this city with its many bridges along which the gondolas are to be seen

14 STILL-LIFE COMPOSITION

Every painter will no doubt have his own method of approach to express his own interpretation of a subject, but, while this is admitted, there must be a certain amount of flexibility in reserve for adjustment to a given type of subject, particularly in still-life.

In the case of a subject where the light is likely to remain consistent for a few hours, there would be less need to jump about the canvas in order to record quickly the fugitive effect of light, therefore the arrangement of the objects will remain the same throughout the painting. This gives plenty of time to choose our objects and arrange our composition. It is always advisable, at the beginning, to select plain items and not such pieces as a special piece of Dresden which, although beautiful and valuable, is quite unsuitable for purposes of study in still-life. The most suitable objects would be all types of bottles (with labels), books, plants in their own pots, various old ginger jars and pieces of various types of plain drapery, not forgetting fruit.

These are the kinds of items which are suitable for arrangement of a composition, a word we should not be terrified by, as the student's own vision is, after all, what matters to him and which will retain his interest. In writing about still-life painting one must avoid treating the exercise as if it were collected like a cooking recipe of different ingredients; while subject matter, drawing, colour and composition are interdependent and cannot be taken and used in separate packets, hence our arrangement or composition.

Let us remember to keep our composition as simple as possible and in the finished painting to be aware of the whole rather than several bits and pieces. An important quality which good works of art have in common without exception is that of unity, and when you attain this there would be control and simplification. This does not mean complication such as a group on a table comprising a plate of fruit, a book, a wineglass, a bottle and an ornamental table lamp with shade – this being illuminated shedding light on the table and leaving the wall behind in shade. This is far from being a simple subject besides the difficulty of portraying the beam of light from an electric bulb, which would be more suitable for an illustration in a monthly magazine.

Unity is normally the first consideration for a good arrangement and should be the first thought of the artist who wishes to set about composing his idea.

Many of the great masters – with few exceptions – have not

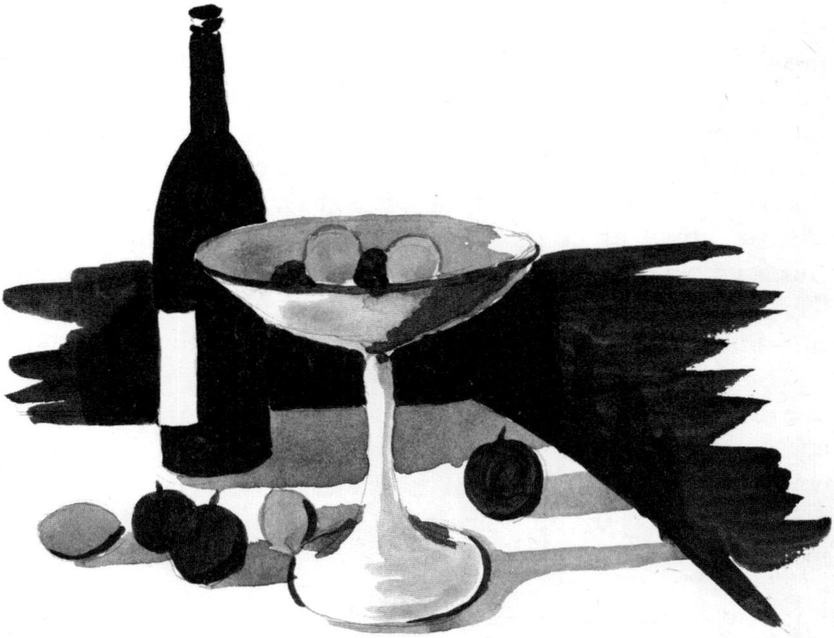

been known for their still-life paintings, most of which have come under the category of simple arrangements, but however few or however many items or masses have been used they all have a coherent whole.

We should have a focal point and a centre of interest which means that we have one picture and not two, an interlacing or overlapping of lines will avoid this. The scale and proportion of the items will help to create interest as well as assisting recession and creating a focal point. The choice of the size of canvas is of great importance, to have the appropriate one available may make the difference between success and failure. Naturally this will be dictated by the subject. Generally a still-life will fit happily on a horizontal shape, but if a plant with flowers is included this will probably require an upright canvas as this adds some dignity to the blooms. If the canvas is too large there will probably be an uncomfortable feeling of emptiness where the area is too large for its content and the painter is tempted to go on with his painting beyond his capabilities. With a smaller area to cover, he will feel a stronger control over his composition and a feeling of enjoyment will have a better chance of being sustained.

In both these groups, Plates 25 and 26, a simple arrangement of commonplace objects has been introduced into each composition where each design is a complete group and not a series of articles making two or three pictures in each scheme. When the objects have been arranged they should have a 'lead in' or a focal point when the items become one whole design.

Colour, too, should have balance and again this is achieved by a small range of colours. In Plate 26, I used Phthalo blue, Burnt umber, Cadmium red, Yellow ochre and Titanium white. The colours in Plate 25 are the same except that Phthalo green was added to introduce the brighter greens in the background and on the book in the foreground. This particular green is often used because of its richer colour and greater scope. Generally speaking a darker and richer colour will often make a lighter colour but a lighter pigment is not easily turned into a dark colour unless you add black, and then the rich colour is immediately ruined.

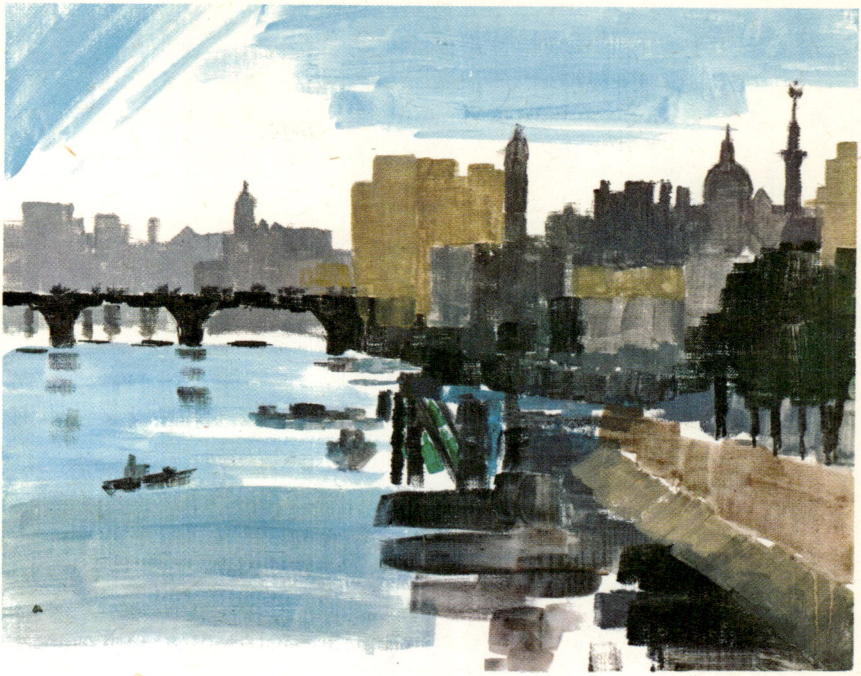

21 An abstract study from London Bridge. The abstraction from the objective study was done in thin Polymer with a wide brush. This produces a more emotional result and particularly when only a small part of the subject is used

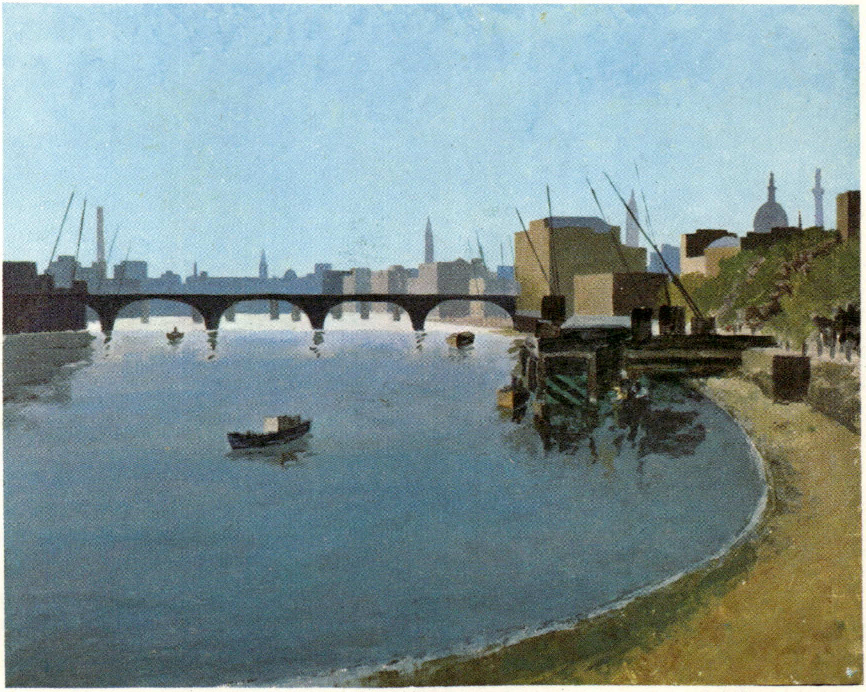

22 London Bridge, River Thames

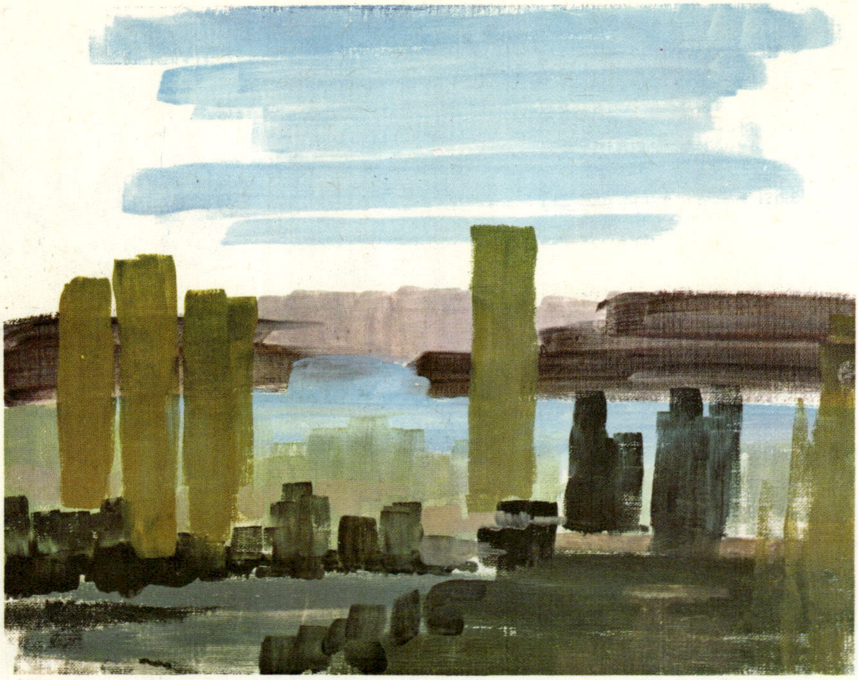

23 Abstract from Plate 24

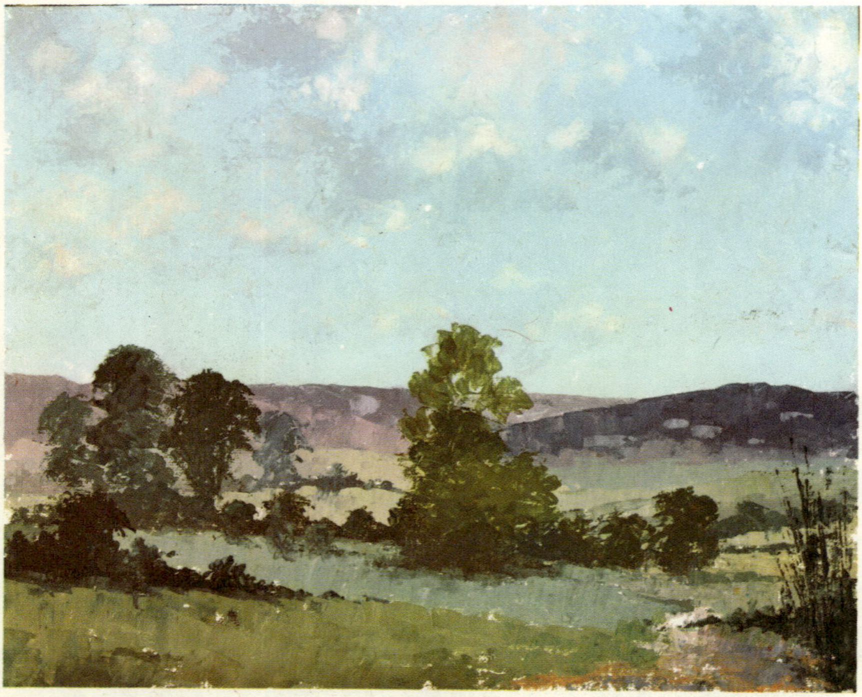

24 Landscape in Kent. The abstract study has been further removed from the design of the Kentish landscape painting. This shows the possibilities when a subject is abstracted

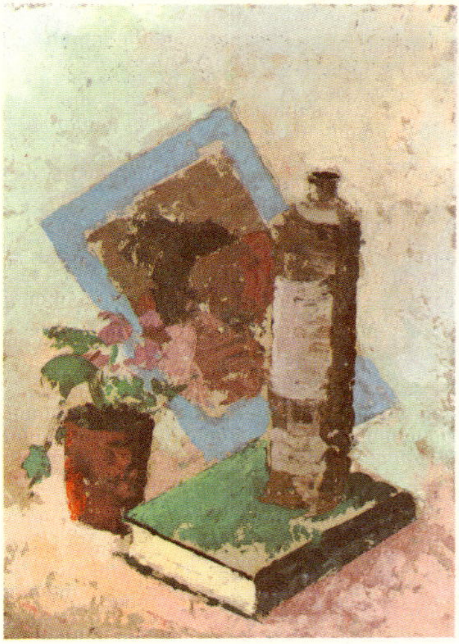

25 Still Life Group.—This was carried out entirely with a palette knife showing the heavy effect of the pigment. The book in the foreground leads the eye towards the composition. The lower subject combines both brush and palette knife and the position of the books leads one into the picture

26 Still Life.—Phthalo blue, Yellow ochre, Burnt umber, Cadmium red, and Titanium white were used for this simple study.

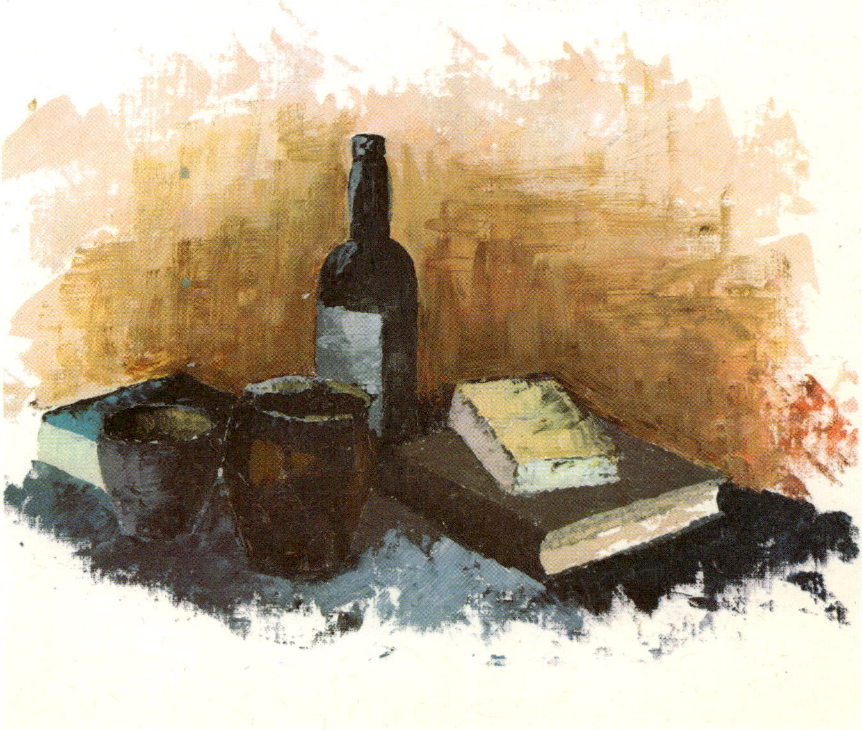

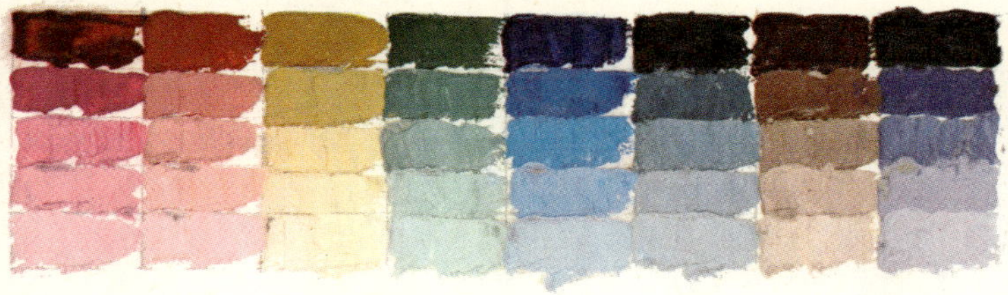

27 Colour Plate showing the use of four colours and some derivatives which are obtainable. The colours used are Alizarin crimson, Alizarin and Yellow ochre, Yellow ochre, Yellow ochre and Phthalo blue, Phthalo blue, Phthalo blue and Burnt umber, Burnt umber, Burnt umber and Alizarin crimson. In each case the colours are reduced with white to indicate the different possibilities

28 Example of using two colours with white—1st colour is Burnt umber, 5th colour is Phthalo green, 2, 3, and 4 are mixtures of the Brown and Green

15 SUGGESTIONS ON COLOUR MIXING

The same question crops up almost every week, 'I'm going on holiday to so-and-so, what colours do I need?' The manufacturer's colour chart shows every conceivable colour, which at first is quite bewildering, but this need not disturb you. Remember all these tints and colours have been made for every type of requirement for all sorts of people – all in need of their own colours to meet their approach to a specific type of work. Because of the wide range of colours in flowers possibly this subject would demand the widest range in order to cover every type of subject whereas in landscape a range of five or six colours would be sufficient. Whatever the subject, and the different type of composition will need its own range of colours, it is a good maxim to remember that a small range of paints will help the unity and harmony more than a very large number. It has often been noticed that when a range of say sixteen colours has been carefully arranged on the palette – which I admit look very attractive – quite half have never been used whilst the others have been reduced to a common denominator. A good example is the number of yellows and reds which are squeezed out, particularly the former where about five colours ranging from Lemon yellow to Raw sienna have been carefully arranged and yet, when they are being used, the student invariably brings them down to a tint resembling pale Yellow ochre or Naples yellow before he uses them.

Whilst all have their own uses, the reds are more precarious and difficult to handle, besides being expensive. The safest in this order, Light red, Cadmium red, Cadmium scarlet and Alizarin crimson should be sufficient for most requirements. Among the blues there is an equally large range and all are somewhat different in their respective tints and origin and enough to satisfy the requirements of everyone no matter what their taste.

Personally I prefer a blue which has a greater range of possibility than another and for this reason I often use Phthalo blue, which is a warm colour and is easily adjusted for different requirements. A dark colour, such as Phthalo blue, which makes a very charming range of light blues with a gradual dilution with white, is preferable to a light blue from which it is impossible to make a dark blue.

A mixture of Phthalo blue and Burnt umber with a little Alizarin will produce an exciting black, equal to any calcinated black, and a pigment which has life in it, particularly if it includes either the umber or the red already in use in the subject. Continuity and unity is more likely to occur than would be the case if, say, Black oxide had been used as this would have a deadening effect on the subject.

Phthalo green, another dark colour, will give an almost unlimited range of light greens when mixed with yellow and white. The brightest would be obtained when mixing with a pale yellow such as a Cadmium yellow and a pale, lower-toned green when Yellow ochre is used. The same rule applies when Phthalo blue is used instead of Phthalo green for the palest greens.

Phthalo blue when mixed with umber will give a dark green as is seen on the dark side of a foreground tree and when a little white is added a very lovely grey-green can be made. To introduce a little more light into this colour a trace of Yellow ochre can be added with more white to represent the light side of the foliage on the tree.

Various mauves can be made by mixing Cadmium red and

Phthalo blue with white; this will give a soft, not too bright mauve. Alizarin crimson mixed with the same blue with white will give a more rich mauve and purple tint. The red which is not suitable for this purpose is Light red and, instead of a clean mauve, it will produce a colour resembling a dirty grey-green. This red however has many other uses, for instance mixed with a little Burnt umber and white a range of colours suitable for brickwork will be created, and Light red mixed with Yellow ochre and white will make a very good flesh colour.

When mixing the lighter tints – particularly the mauves and greens – always begin by taking the white first and gradually adding the other colours to it only a little at a time. If you mix the other way round you will end up with enough colour to paint the whole house or use up all your white, ending with a great heap of paint which may have to be scraped away. Only experience will tell you how much to mix and how not to waste good paint. A good guide to the amount of white to begin with would be a lump about the size of a butter bean and the smallest trace of the desired colour added. Remember you can always add more but not take away.

Develop the habit of mixing with the palette knife – it mixes better and saves ruining your brushes; it is also easy to clean and wipe on your rag. Brushes need more rinsing in water and after a while they soon lose their shape with this sort of treatment. Anyway, brushes are for painting with and not for mixing paint.

Every artist has his own choice of colours which from experience have proved suitable to his own requirements – this gives each of them a distinguishable quality which is associated with his work – some may wish to express their thoughts with high-keyed 'Fauve'-type colour whereas another will always see his work in lower-toned harmonies. Provided the work has a satisfactory harmony or contrast and the unity preserves a balance of form it becomes a matter of personal taste.

A suitable list of colours to cover most subjects is: Cadmium yellow, Yellow ochre, Burnt umber, Cadmium red, Cadmium scarlet, Alizarin crimson, Phthalo blue, Phthalo green, Cerulean blue and Titanium white.

16 MORE ADVICE AND WHAT TO AVOID

The advantages of Polymer painting are numerous and easily understood.

When using the paint it is best to mix it on a 'palette' of glass, Perspex or Formica and not on an absorbent surface like a wood palette. One about fifteen inches by ten inches is a suitable size.

Almost any surface is suitable for painting on, either canvas, canvas board, hardboard, or any slightly absorbent surface can be used. Any unprepared surface can be used and a mixture of thinned (with water) Polymer may be applied which will dry ready for use in about half an hour. If a coloured ground is preferred use a coloured pigment instead of white.

Sometimes you may wish to use an old oil painting which may be prepared in the same way either for painting again with oil colours or continuing with the Polymer paint. It can be used either way provided the paint underneath is dry.

If the paint is to be used thinly brushes are quite useful but if thick heavy pigment is being used, a palette knife will be found the most useful and it is also easy to clean.

All the colours are in transparent tubes so the colour remains visible even if the label becomes unreadable.

Remember always to replace the cap after taking out some colour, if not the pigment will harden owing to its quick-drying properties. If the cap has not been screwed on fully the paint

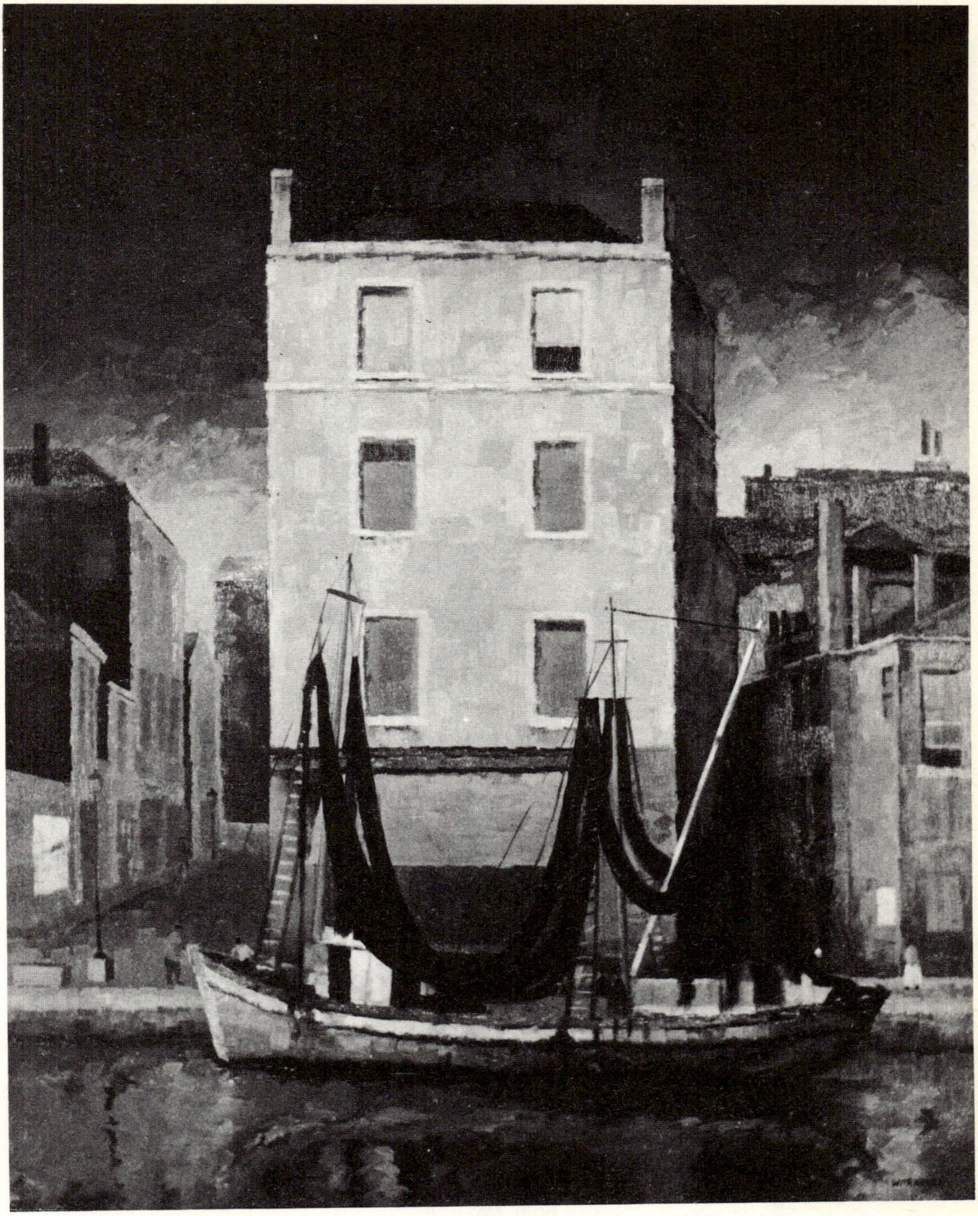

'The Moorings'—In the collection of Douglas Yates, Esq. The curve of the drying nets gives added importance to the composition when shown against the rigidity of the white house

will harden in the neck of the tube and some difficulty may be noticed, in about a week, in taking off the cap. If this should happen heat the top with a match or a lighter and the cap will unscrew. To soften the paint inside the tube, push something like a nail into the tube and make a long hole and then fill this with the Polymer medium or water and screw the cap on securely. This should be soft and ready for use by the next day.

Do not leave any old paint on the palette after use but clean off and wash in hot water, ready for use the next day.

If you wish to varnish your work the next day, use only the medium provided and not any other ordinary varnish. Normally the paint dries with an eggshell finish, quite evenly and without any trace of unevenness or sinking, and is equally permanent without varnishing.

Because the paint dries quickly, don't get alarmed and run into a panic allowing the paint to get out of control. You must remember to hold back the drying by adding water to the colours on your palette and keep it within your own control. In other words, learn to understand it and modify its particular features to your own requirements and expression. Although the paint dries quickly this is often an advantage, as it allows one to paint on an already dry surface, without waiting for a few days for it to dry, and the succeeding work will not show any change in appearance as it would in other media.

When you start to sketch in your subject, this can be done with a small brush using thin colour like watercolour or you may prefer to use a pencil; either will be suitable, but if you use charcoal for your drawing remember to use a fixative to stop the black mixing with your paint. This can make what you thought was a light sky look rather sad and dirty.

When Polymer is used in warmer conditions, such as obtain in Italy, Spain or similar hot countries during the summer months, it will be found helpful to select a shady position in order to keep the hot sun from the sketch.

The importance of keeping the paint soft cannot be over-emphasised. Frequent drops of water added to the colour should keep the paint moist.

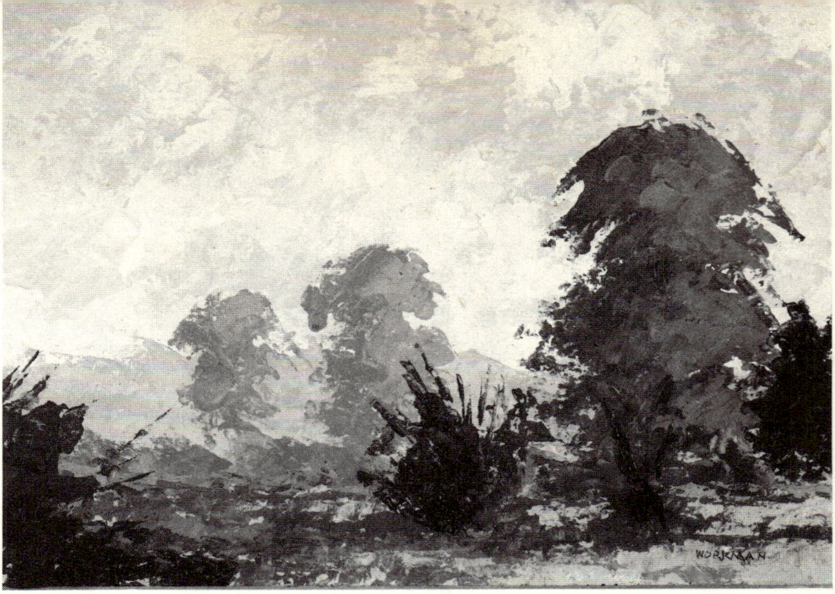

A study of trees and scrubland carried out with a palette knife

It is also a useful tip, when the work is finished, to add a few drops of water to each tube before screwing on the cap. This will help future use by preventing the pigment from getting hard.

Frequently I have been asked, do I like this new paint and do I use it? My answer is always the same – I love it!

'Dull Day, River Teign, Devon'

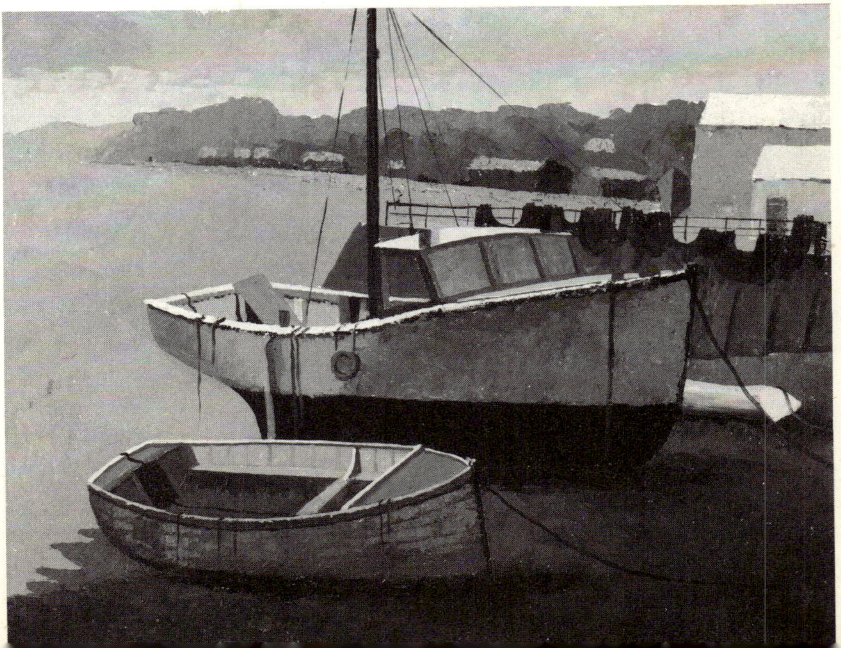

FINAL REMARKS

For obvious reasons, the students at many Art Colleges have found that Polymer paint has become a 'must' in their equipment and studies: whether it is in the Mural School, Interior Decoration or general Painting Studies it is always to be found in use for different purposes.

The Teacher Training Colleges find it most helpful in their art studies for the training of the teacher of the future.

Architects and Interior Designers use it for their work because of its richness and quick-drying properties.

Professional artists are aware of its usefulness for every form of painting, either indoor or outdoor, for sketching or finished work as well as being a suitable under-painting. In every case where this technical understanding has been achieved and a pictorial result maintained it has been artistically approved and accepted. A special value in studio work is in its opacity and evenness when it dries on art boards and gloss surfaces.

Generally, because of its particular qualities and adaptability, it has assisted in enlarging the artist's possibilities and expression. His work has greatly benefited by this technical development.

Nearly two thousand years ago painters were dependent either on earth colours or the grinding of precious stones into powder which were then suspended in oil, but today science has presented us with a pigment equally permanent and filled with lustre.